Practitioner's Guide to Operationalizing Data Governance

Wiley and SAS Business Series

The Wiley and SAS Business Series presents books that help senior level managers with their critical management decisions.

Titles in the Wiley and SAS Business Series include:

For more information on any of the above titles, please visit www.wiley.com.

Practitioner's Guide to Operationalizing Data Governance

Mary Anne Hopper

WILEY

Library of Congress Cataloging-in-Publication Data:

Names: Hopper, Mary Anne, author.
Title: Practitioner's guide to operationalizing data governance / Mary Anne Hopper.
Description: Hoboken, New Jersey : Wiley, [2023] | Series: Wiley and SAS business series | Includes index.
Identifiers: LCCN 2023001522 (print) | LCCN 2023001523 (ebook) | ISBN 9781119851424 (cloth) | ISBN 9781119851455 (adobe pdf) | ISBN 9781119851431 (epub)
Subjects: LCSH: Database management. | Management information systems—Management. | Data integrity.
Classification: LCC QA76.9.D3 H6564 2023 (print) | LCC QA76.9.D3 (ebook) | DDC 005.75/65—dc23/eng/20230201
LC record available at https://lccn.loc.gov/2023001522
LC ebook record available at https://lccn.loc.gov/2023001523

Cover Design: Wiley
Cover Image: © shulz/Getty Images

SKY10044710_032023

For the MAC team (Faramarz, Matthias, Matt, Katie, Noah, and Liz) for all your support

and

For Bill for never letting me throw the term "best practice" out there without explaining "the why".

Contents

Acknowledgments

A methodology does not create itself overnight. It takes time, encouragement, and dedication from a lot of people. The methodology I have laid out for you is from the work and guidance of my colleagues at the SAS Institute: Faramarz Abedini, Matthias Gruber, Robert Stone, Matt Benson, Katie Lorenze, Noah Pearce, and Liz Baker. Some of you I have worked with for many years, some not quite as long. Either way, your fingerprints are embedded in the content of these pages. For that, I thank you!

CHAPTER **1**

Introduction

INTENDED AUDIENCE

As long as the practice of Data Governance has been around, the concept continues to lack sustainable adoption in many organizations. My main objective with this book is to share my experience and help you and your organization on your journey, no matter where in that journey you are.

My best guess is that you are looking at this book as a guide for one of the following reasons:

- Your organization is thinking about Data Governance.
- You have been tasked with Data Governance.
- You need to get your Data Governance program back on track.
- You have acquired a tool and want to get the most value from your investment.
- You continue to have the same data quality issues over and over.
- You attended a conference and learned about Data Governance and think it is something you need.

The content in this book is meant for a large audience because Data Governance impacts the entire organization. Whether a senior leader or an individual contributor, you may be asked to participate at some level in Data Governance, actively or passively.

This book guides you through practical steps in applying Data Governance concepts to solve business problems by adopting a disciplined approach to Data Management methods. The chapters cover prioritization, alignment of Data Governance and Data Management, organizational structures, defining roles and responsibilities, communications, measurements, operations, implementation, and policies. All of the examples presented are not conceptual; they are real-world customer examples that can be applied to your specific organization.

EXPERIENCE

You most likely have an interest in not just Data Governance, but in data itself. Do you remember your "Aha" moment that turned you into a data junkie? I remember mine clearly. In the early 1990s, I worked for a small naval architectural firm. The focus of the firm was primarily custom high-end racing sailboat designs, including the America's Cup. One day my boss brought in a floppy disk and asked me to take a look at what was on it. Apparently, we had a client who thought his brand-new boat was slow. The disk contained the data dump from the boat's instruments. There were fields like time of day, heading, wind velocity, and boat speed. I was able to parse the data and essentially recreate the races with the available data points. What I learned was that the boat tacked nine or ten times on the first leg of each race. I know not all of you are expert sailboat racers but take my word for it; tacking that many times on any leg of a race in a big boat is slow. What did that mean for my boss? He was able to have a different conversation with our client. We were no longer defending boat design or building materials but instead talking about racing tactics and offering suggestions for improvements there first.

That day changed my view of the power of data and from that point forward I chose classes and career roles that were focused on data. Initially, I focused on database development and support and then transitioned into data warehouse development. On the IT side, I managed the development of platforms to support finance and treasury processes as well as the re-platforming of a home-grown loan servicing system. That experience enlightened me to the need for data quality processes and the understanding of data lineage and documented business rules. There came a time when I transitioned into project management, product ownership, and finally consulting. The consulting role is what has helped me most in hearing customer challenges and helping them solve those problems by instilling discipline in Data Management processes.

Over the years, I have worked with hundreds of clients across all industry verticals to help them establish that discipline in Data Management practices. In other words, helping them to establish Data Governance programs that align with their individual organization's business objectives while also considering their maturity, culture, and appetite for Data Governance.

This book is not only a reflection of a tested and proven methodology but also my experiences in what works and what doesn't work, things to not get hung up on, and where best to focus efforts. Some of the chapters are shorter than others but I still believe the topics are important enough to cover. My hope is that this book helps you and your organization in your own Data Governance journey.

COMMON CHALLENGE THEMES

Most of what I've heard over the years can be broken down into a set of common themes. One of the best ways to talk about those themes is to share with you what I've heard my clients say. Every quote is directly from a customer. If any of these quotes resonate with you, then formalizing Data Governance can help. You will see these themes again in future chapters.

Metadata

 Metadata is the practice of gathering, storing, and provisioning information about data assets. As important as it is to collect and maintain, it is a practice that does not formally exist in most organizations. Most of my customers might not necessarily use the term metadata, but the concept is top of mind for them. There is a desire to have common terms defined and have a single repository to maintain information about those terms. Because there is no formal metadata process or repository, users spend a lot of their time trying to understand data on their own or relying on others to interpret meaning for them. Another byproduct from the lack of metadata process is that users complain of not knowing what data is available to them. Always keep in mind that metadata is a precursor to data quality; I will write more about that topic in later chapters.

Here is what clients have said:

- ▪ "we need Rosetta Stone for our data"
- ▪ "metadata is so important and it doesn't exist"
- ▪ "the most time-consuming part is to find what you're looking for"
- ▪ "would be nice to follow the trail"
- ▪ "can't get to confident decisions without common definitions"

- "a little bit of detective work and a little bit of knowledge"
- "this is what I mean when I say 'this'"
- "we haven't the foggiest idea of what the denominator is"
- "you get the data and it's not what you meant"
- "some people just want to call it something different"

Access to Data

 Oftentimes, there are very few people with the "know-how" and the tools to access data. Users who do have direct access feel they must navigate a labyrinth to get to the data they need. That labyrinth includes multiple reports, accessing tables, or calling people who have knowledge of data structures. Because of this, users find it easier to maintain their own datasets instead of accessing a common repository. In most organizations, users are anxious to have access to tools to make it easier to use data.

Here is what clients have said:

- "we got to know what the hell we got"
- "our issue isn't so much storage, it's access"
- "quit parking data on some machine"
- "a whole lot of horsepower to pull data out of that system"
- "you have to have your DNA tested before you get access to it"
- "not knowing something exists is a greater liability than not using what is available"
- "a lot of what we're doing seems so hard"
- "information does not seem readily available"
- "manual data exercise to put it together"
- "we have so much information out there in so many places"
- "Excel becomes the big workhorse"
- "we've created a process to deal with lack of access to information"
- "want to hire an analyst, not a SQL person"
- "high-priced analyst just getting data for people"

Trust in Data

 Users want the ability to make solid decisions on trusted data that is deemed a definitive source of truth. However, users feel there is a lack of consistency across data sources. Some of the reasons for this could be related to data latency, poor data collection practices, a lack of data understanding (e.g., data acceptance, service level agreements, data remediation, and data profiling), or different groups creating and maintaining their own copies of data. This results in users feeling they spend a significant amount of time validating or defending the data they do use.

Here is what clients have said:

- "depending on which query you run you get a different answer"
- "can't create individual sources of truth"
- "the place we pull the data from doesn't balance to itself"
- "we don't know how reliable the data is"
- "you trust the data until you know it's not right"
- "if you can't fix the problem you work around it"
- "how do we know what an error looks like?"

Data Integration

 Data integration consists of processes for moving and combining data that reside in multiple locations and providing a unified view of the data. In many environments, users who need access to integrated data are essentially required to pull several reports or datasets and then integrate on their desktop using MS Access or Excel. There may also be a lack of formal processes or tool usage across divisions and even in IT. More often than not, this results in differing business rules that are applied to data, which turns into discrepancies in the data results.

Here is what clients have said:

- "I'm living in spreadsheet hell"
- "really no linking it all together"

- "right now, it's fragmented"
- "all our stuff doesn't talk to each other"
- "being able to stitch data together is what we need"
- "our systems have never been organized to allow us to answer questions"
- "almost every prototype that we did last fiscal year had to do with the difficulty of pulling data from multiple datasets"
- "we have a lot of questions, we have a lot of data, but we can't pull it out easily"

Data Ownership

 Users do not know who to contact when there are data questions. There is a desire to have a named data owner for the various domains who can answer questions, address issues, and help users understand data usage guidelines for given datasets.

Here is what clients have said:

- "you're stepping on toes every time you go in there"
- "everybody wants to control their own fate"
- "that's our data so we should be able to keep up with it"
- "lack of accountability for data responsibility"
- "we don't really know who does that"

Reporting/Analytics

 Users are becoming more data aware. Although some users only require operational reports, there is a growing curiosity and desire for more advanced analytic capabilities. This makes the reporting and analytic platform (e.g., data warehouse, data mart, date lake, etc.) being part of the overall strategic plan more important than ever. Most users feel it takes up a lot of their time to get reports and like the concept of a single point of entry for all of their reports as opposed to reports within the various applications that they are forced to self-integrate.

Here is what clients have said:

- "how much of that data is relevant to the next level of the department?"
- "I don't think people realize what we could do [if our data were integrated]"
- "very myopic view of the data"
- "[we need to be able to provide] reliable, repeatable answers to questions"
- "the most time-consuming part is to find what you're looking for"
- "would like to have a dashboard to share accurate information"
- "it's more art than science"
- "information is perceived as ad-hoc"
- "used to managing without information"
- "too much reliance on old data to make current decisions"

Data Architecture

 While most organizations have an architecture practice in place, the teams often lack authority because they do not have a formally defined charter. There is no formal data strategy to help set the team's direction and enable it to define standards and guidelines for identifying, provisioning, storing, and integrating data. With newly formed teams especially, the focus is on new applications instead of the entire enterprise data landscape that has been growing for years with no formal practices in place.

Here is what clients have said:

- "there have been so many architecture hands over the years"
- "we are duplicating a lot of information"
- "[there is] no logic in how we approach managing data"
- "data should be accessible regardless of where its source is"
- "it's extremely laborious"
- "tendency to work like we're all artisans here"

- "by the time you figure out what everyone else is doing it becomes faster to do it yourself"
- "we're on the bleeding edge of end of life"
- "[it takes] a whole lot of horsepower to pull data"

Reliance on Individual Knowledge

 I cannot remember the last time I was with a customer who did not feel overly reliant on go-to people to help them with understanding, getting at, or validating data or reports. Many of the things I talk about in this section are symptoms of an "I know a guy/gal" culture that becomes embedded in the organization because of a lack of a shared data dictionary, unknown data quality, difficulty in accessing data or reports, or an inconsistent data architecture.

Here is what clients have said:

- "a little bit of detective work and a little bit of knowledge"
- "if I need the data, so and so can whip me up a SQL query"
- "it's a fishing expedition to find people who can get you information"
- "not everybody knows everybody"
- "need to unlock the creativity of the bright people in our organization"
- "I should be able to run my reports"

Culture

 Kicking off a Data Governance program or breathing new life into an existing program will more than likely require a culture shift. This can be one of the largest hurdles in overall sustainability of your program. This culture shift usually involves two things. The first is communicating across division or line of business silos. Communication involves everything from policies to policy compliance reporting to program performance. The second is in data sharing. I am often told that people want access to data not created in their focus area, but others just do not want to grant access because they are data hoarders. More often than not, I find that people are reluctant to share because they are afraid of how the data may possibly be misused or misinterpreted.

Here is what clients have said:

- "[we are] great at planning but fall short on implementation"
- "divisions operate within their own zones"
- "we have a culture of independence and resistance"
- "[there will] always be people out there doing crazy s**t"
- "we're beyond 'it would be nice to have'"
- "lots of good people who do lots of good work"
- "we have departments where all they do is protect themselves against bad data"
- "we don't teach data awareness"
- "focus a lot of our measures on things that are easy"
- "what we do is reactive"

HOW DATA GOVERNANCE CAN HELP

Let's think about the themes again, and I will provide some examples of how Data Governance can help. There is definitely cross-over in some of these areas. For example, providing metadata to users will help with data access challenges in better understanding what data is available for use.

Metadata

 Data Governance provides the process for collecting, updating, storing, and provisioning. A metadata policy will contain not just the process but what attribution should be collected about what data in the environment. This helps users because they have access to common business terms (rationalized across different sources) and some sort of consolidated and updated data dictionary. I will explore metadata in more detail in Chapter 5, Common Starting Points, and Chapter 13, Policies.

Access to Data

The Data Governance organization may not own a policy for data access but can provide the communication mechanism for standards with regard to how users will access data resources. Modes of access may be through common tools or interfaces and be dependent on user roles and skill sets. With these policies in place, users will enjoy easier access to data with data access tools as well as a better understanding of what is in the data ecosystem for their use.

Trust in Data

This is a central component of any Data Governance program as data quality is top of mind for all users. A data quality policy will include processes and standards for data profiling, data acceptance, remediation, continuous monitoring, and reporting. A solid data quality process builds trust between data and users. Instead of defending definitions and applied business rules, analysts can actually spend their time interpreting the results of analyses to inform future decisions. Like metadata, data quality will be specifically addressed in the Common Starting Points and Policies chapters.

Data Integration

Policies and standards can be developed to ensure consistent practices when it comes to integrating data across multiple tables or schemas. These policies are typically developed and maintained by some type of Data Management team, but they are Data Governance policies, nonetheless. A Data Governance organization may require the policies, and once established, developers can be more consistent in developing reusable components that can be more easily updated or maintained. Standards may also define what tools are used for data integration and business rule development.

Data Ownership

 Like a lot of other words in the Data Governance space, Data Owner means different things to different people. One of the key outputs of a Data Governance program is defining roles and responsibilities. Whether or not a role is called Data Owner, there will be a role that users understand to be their go-to person. This reduces angst with users and saves them time when they have questions about a particular dataset, report result, or even just a general question. This role can also help establish data usage guidelines so other users understand what they can and cannot do with certain pieces of data.

Reporting/Analytics

 Data Governance policies can document changes to business rules or external data impacts, which might be necessary to provide relevant context to data users. An example might be the need to know when legislative policy changes take place. In addition, standards might define what tools which users will utilize to build or access reports or datasets. These standards provide consistency and ensure reliability of analyses and reports. It should go without saying that metadata and data quality are necessary components to support robust reporting and analytic platforms.

Data Architecture

 Data architecture is foundational to understanding what data is, where it is stored, how it is moved across different systems, and how it is integrated (yes, data integration). Data architecture policies include standards for data modeling, naming, and ETL processes. Having these policies in place helps to ensure more scalable, repeatable solutions that reduce development efforts because of consistency across datasets and reusability of data and code.

Reliance on Individual Knowledge

While there will not be a specific Data Governance policy to address this topic, a maturing Data Governance program will reduce individual reliance because there are policies and processes that address metadata and data quality as well as defined roles and responsibilities. The end goal here is to create as much of a self-sustaining data ecosystem as is feasible for a given organization.

Culture

Like the reliance on individual knowledge, Data Governance will not create and maintain policies, processes, or standards that address an organization's culture. The culture shift becomes a byproduct of having the other policies in place. For example, when there are policies in place (that you are compliant with) that address metadata, there will be less ambiguity about data assets and users will understand what data means so they are less likely to inadvertently misinterpret a definition. That in itself leads to breaking down division silos and promotes data sharing. That becomes a win-win across an organization.

Chapter 1 - Introduction Summary

I have given you a welcome, shared my experience, and explored common themes and how Data Governance can help solve those problems. In closing, I offer a short overview for each of the upcoming chapters. You can read straight through or choose a topic that is of particular interest to you.

Chapter 2 - Rethinking Data Governance

This chapter will explore popular approaches to Data Governance and walk you through a high-level disciplined approach to planning, designing, and launching a program. Other chapters will detail the concepts outlined in this chapter.

Chapter 3 - Data Governance and Data Management

I will share a detailed framework for Data Governance and Data Management that includes Data Governance, Data Management, Data Stewardship, Business Drivers, Solutions, and Methods. Each component of the framework will be described in detail.

Chapter 4 - Priorities

In order to be successful in Data Governance, you need to have focus. I will share with you prioritization approaches. By the way, these work for non–Data Governance–related activities as well.

Chapter 5 - Common Starting Points

The most common starting points for Data Governance are metadata and data quality. I will talk about these two concepts in detail as I expect they will be foundational to your program.

Chapter 6 - Data Governance Planning

Data Governance planning begins with defined program objectives. They are truly the cornerstone for program activities, defining roles and responsibilities, measuring and monitoring, and communication. I will provide guidance as well as examples for creating objectives. Guiding principles are also important in that they provide direction for a program. Like objectives, I will provide examples you can use as a starting point.

Chapter 7 - Organizational Framework

When asking people to participate in Data Governance, they need to understand what they are going to be tasked with doing and how their role fits into an overall ecosystem. I will provide several examples of organizational frameworks and give tips for creating one for your organization.

Chapter 8 - Roles and Responsibilities

After defining an organizational framework, you need to be able to define activities and decisions (that align to defined objectives) and then align them to said organizational framework so there is no confusion about who is doing what. I will provide examples and talk about the process of creating detailed responsibilities so you can take the next logical step of naming names.

Chapter 9 - Operating Procedures

Data Governance participants will be curious, and sometimes anxious, about what it looks like to participate in the program. I will share samples of detailed operating procedures along with sample workflows that represent program to-do's, which were derived from the roles and responsibilities.

Chapter 10 - Communication

Communication is an important Data Governance program management function. This chapter will explore the key components of a communication plan provide and provide a sample.

Chapter 11 - Measurement

Establishing measures for both policy compliance and program progress are important. This chapter will provide measures that are aligned to program objectives. I will also share a program scorecard you can use as a starting point.

Chapter 12 - Roadmap

It is difficult to measure and communicate program progress without a plan in place. The roadmap needs to be aligned to implementation of the organizational framework. I will talk about key workstreams and how they can be reflected in a program roadmap. The sample roadmap can be used as a starting point, or even to help you determine cadence.

Chapter 13 - Policies

This chapter discusses the different components of a Data Governance policy. It also provides two policy examples (one for metadata, the other for data quality) you can use as starting points. The policies are annotated with special considerations for why decisions were made.

Chapter 14 - Data Governance Maturity

This final chapter will provide a recap and summarize Data Governance concepts as it explores how to mature your Data Governance program.

CHAPTER 2

Rethinking Data Governance

RESULTS YOU CAN EXPECT WITH COMMON APPROACHES TO DATA GOVERNANCE

Let's take a closer look at some of the common approaches to Data Governance and why they ultimately fail. Some of these might sound familiar to you.

Here Comes Panera

This is one of the most popular approaches to Data Governance I've seen. A group of people get together to form a Data Governance program. One of the participant's managers thinks it is a great idea and orders lunch for everyone. The Panera Bread lunch spread shows up with the salad, dressing, sandwiches (turkey, roast beef, and veggie), cookies, and sodas or water. The group begins to air their data grievances. Someone takes notes and enters a "list" into an Excel spreadsheet. The meeting typically lasts about 2½ hours. The participants leave excited that they have a list of "issues" that need to be addressed and agree to meet again in a month. The month goes by, and the group reconvenes. But this time there is no lunch spread, only the cookies and sodas/waters. The conversation is exactly the same as it was the first time around. But still, the group leaves pretty excited. Another month goes by. The group meets again but this time two things are different. The first is someone brought a little bag of Hershey chocolate bars. The second is not as many people have shown up. Data Governance is already a failing endeavor.

Why does this approach not work? Because in order for people to want to continue participating in a Data Governance program they need to feel like they are both making decisions and making a difference. A better strategy would be to take the "list" and turn it into a set of measurable objectives. That way, participants have an identified set of common goals.

Case in point, I worked with a customer (actually, a lot of customers) who told me they started Data Governance so many times with this approach that the only reason people show up is for the kick-off lunch. Some of these organizations have also admitted they cannot use the term "Data Governance" anymore because of organizational fatigue with starting something that was doomed from the get-go.

Voluntelling

Someone in a leadership position decides that a Data Governance program is a good idea. Perhaps they are tired of numbers from different reports not matching. Perhaps they read an article and it sounded like something they should take on. Perhaps there is a mandate from an audit. Regardless of the reason, the leader thinks it is a good idea so they "voluntell" several folks in their reporting structure to "go and do" Data Governance. There may even be a Panera Bread spread at a kick-off for the Data Governance effort.

Why does this approach not work? Because there is a lack of overall business value alignment. Data Governance needs a purpose beyond doing it just to do it. This is especially true when organizational boundaries and reporting structures need to be crossed.

Case in point, I worked with a large bank in South America. The Chief Data Officer said she had established roles, but felt most of her time was spent "herding cats." I asked if she had defined program objectives that were aligned to overall business objectives with dedicated and defined roles and responsibilities. She said that had not been done. Well, nobody knew what was expected of them and everyone appointed to a Data Governance role had their own perception of what needed to be done.

Misaligning Titles and Roles

An organization decides it is time to create roles to better serve the needs of the organization. The first step might be to create a reporting team to consolidate data and reporting requests. The idea is that if the team is co-located, they will be better at communicating with each other and the byproduct will be streamlined delivery as well as more consistent results. The folks on the team even get updated titles or designations such as Data Steward, Data Custodian, Data Trustee, or even Data Owner.

Why does this approach not work? Because solely granting some- one a title does not mean that they a) know what work comes with the title, and b) necessarily have the organizational authority to accompany the title. Data Governance requires defined roles and responsibilities and named resources that are aligned to authority. If the people do not understand their role, they will simply ignore it or you end up with an organization full of "titles" that operate differently. That is sure con- fusing for the rest of the organization. Or you appoint people to roles where they have no authority, and others will simply work around them. Both reasons are doomed.

Case in point, while working with a records management com- pany, they had no Data Governance program in place yet they had identified more than 100 Data Stewards. I pried and found out that when new hires took online Cognos training and completed an add- on module, they became a Data Steward. In this organization, report writers were granted a title that was completely misaligned with their actual role. And, when people called them because they were Data Stewards, they were completely ineffective. Data Governance had not even started and it was already deemed a failure.

Project Delivery

There is a new enterprise initiative. It could be an ERP implementation. It could be CRM. It could be Customer 360. It could be a new analytic platform. It actually doesn't matter. Any of these types of projects have data, and eventually somebody is going to want to look at that data. As part of the scope of one of these projects, Data Governance gets added in and somebody is tasked with collecting some metadata and making decisions about user roles. Data Governance is off and running.

Why does this approach not work? Because projects end. And when they end, the project resources move on to their next assign- ment. The byproduct is that anything that was implemented to support the project runs a big risk of becoming stale or outdated.

Case in point, I worked with an organization who established Data Stewardship as part of a master data management implementation. The Data Stewards were part of the project team, and once the project ended, there was no ongoing responsibility to review the exceptions.

A short time passed, and suddenly there were thousands of records with exceptions based on the criteria established by the project and no one to review them.

Tool Deployment

Your organization just invested in a tool to support functions like metadata, data lineage, or data quality. The investment could be for a given department or for the entire enterprise. The tool is implemented and branded as Data Governance. Oftentimes, the technology is owned by a technology group with little to no business input or ongoing involvement. The teams create or import metadata, create data quality reports, and develop data remediation processes. Participation in Data Governance activities is optional.

Why does this approach not work? There is no true understanding of what problems were going to be solved with the tool. Data Governance needs defined objectives. Those objectives should drive the requirements for the tool. In other words, build the organizational structure first, then ask if you have the tools to help you meet those objectives.

Case in point, I worked with a grocery chain and met with a team of Data Quality Analysts whose biggest complaint was they spent all their time creating and publishing data quality reports that nobody ever acted on unless they kept the store from selling a product. It turned out that there were no processes or defined roles and responsibilities. Any actions were a courtesy, not a requirement.

WHAT DOES WORK

Adopting Consistent Definitions

I've learned two things about people's perceptions of Data Governance over the years. The first is that it means different things to different people. To some it means data quality. To others it means to create a spreadsheet and identify all the data elements in use across the data ecosystem. To others it is the implementation of a set of tools to solve a very tactical issue such as data quality, data security, or to build a business data glossary. Still, to others it becomes a catch-all for a way to solve every problem in an organization. The second is that it becomes a catch-all for any and all problems across an organization. The Data Governance program is meant to promote the oversight of data assets. Data Governance does not have a role in common challenges such as project delivery processes, resourcing needs, IT project prioritization, or establishment of business objectives.

The important thing to remember is that the group of people taking on the Data Governance endeavor, whether they are executives or part of a grassroots effort, need to align around a common definition for Data Governance. Here is my favorite definition: *Data Governance is the organizational framework establishing strategy, objectives, and policies for shared data assets.* This definition reflects the necessity of people and processes. In other words, Data Governance is a group of people who are part of decision making to set policies, procedures, and standards and provide oversight and discipline to achieve desired and measurable data management outcomes.

Disciplined Approach to Program Planning, Design, and Execution

If we are asking people to come together to make decisions and communicate about data, they need to know what is expected of them. Defining what is expected of participants takes some effort. The details of that effort are the focus of future chapters. At the highest level, I like to break down the effort into three manageable steps: Plan, Design, Execute. Let's take a look at what I mean by each of these steps.

 Plan

Planning is taking the list of challenges (perhaps created during the Panera Bread kick-off lunch) and then establishing scope, defining a set of objectives, guiding principles, decision-making bodies (organizational framework), and high-level decision-making rights. These topics are covered in detail in the following chapters: Priorities, Common Starting Points, Data Governance Planning, and Organizational Framework.

Design

After defining the organizational structure that will help meet program objectives, you need to think about how the program is going to operate. I recommend being prescriptive at first and then letting participants define what works best for them once they "practice." To-do's included in this step are defining key activities and decisions, assigning decision-making authority, developing operating procedures, designing key workflows, developing a communication plan, defining program metrics, developing a participant and onboarding strategy, and building an overall program roadmap. The end of this step can include identifying key participants. I call that last one out separately because a lot of organizations jump to this step before thinking about what the participants are going to be asked to do (take a look back at the previous section). These topics are covered in detail in the following chapters: Roles and Responsibilities, Communication, Measurement, and Strategy/Roadmap.

Execute

Execute is exactly as it sounds. This is the official launch of your program as you begin to execute against the program roadmap. At the beginning of this step, time is spent with onboarding, training, and policy development and approval. Policies are key to any Data Governance program. There are samples in the Policies chapter. As the program matures, the reach of the program can be expanded and Data Governance moves away from mostly establishing policies to monitoring them, reporting, and communicating.

RETHINKING DATA GOVERNANCE SUMMARY

After reading the first section of this chapter, you may have thought "that's us, we're doomed!" You are not. Your program is not. No matter the state of your program, you can always take a step back and reorganize. But you need to reorganize in a disciplined and methodical manner. I encourage you to read on and apply what follows to your program.

CHAPTER 3

Data Governance and Data Management

RESULTS YOU CAN EXPECT FOCUSING PURELY ON DATA GOVERNANCE OR DATA MANAGEMENT

Data Governance and Data Management need to work hand-in-hand. Data Governance provides the oversight, measurement, and communication while Data Management provides the tactical operations to achieve desired outcomes. You can sit down and write policies, but if there is no measurable result that helps to meet a desired outcome, it is nothing but an academic exercise. Those programs will fail. Likewise, Data Management with no discipline or oversight continues a "wild west" culture and data environments that will only get harder to maintain and expand over time. Those programs will fail.

SAS DATA MANAGEMENT FRAMEWORK

It is important to understand how Data Governance and Data Management align in support of larger business goals. A great first step to gaining this understanding is to examine an overall framework of a program and its components parts. They can be broken down into Data Governance, Data Management, Data Stewardship, Business Drivers, Solutions, and Methods. The SAS Data Management Framework shown below breaks down each of these components. After reading and understanding the different components, you are better poised to have conversations with others about how Data Governance and Data Management when aligned as part of an overall program can help improve the overall data ecosystem (Figure 3.1).

Business Drivers				
Customer Focus	Compliance Mandates	Mergers & Acquisitions	Decision Making	Operational Efficiencies

Data Governance	Data Stewardship	Data Management	
Program Objectives		Data Architecture	Data Administration
Guiding Principles		Data Quality	Metadata
Decision-Making Bodies		Data Lifecycle	Data Security
Decision Rights		Reporting & Analytics	Reference & Master Data

Methods	Solutions					
People	Data Cleansing	Business Intelligence	Data Visualization	Data Integration	Machine Learning	Artificial Intelligence
Process						
Technology	Data Monitoring	Data Lineage	Data Profiling	Metadata Repository	Data Catalog	Master Data Management

Figure 3.1 SAS Data Management Framework.

Data Governance

I am repeating the definition I gave you earlier. Data Governance is *the organizational framework for establishing strategy, objectives, and policies for enterprise or shared data*. Successful programs have something in common. They take the time to define measurable objectives, guiding principles (or guardrails), decision-making bodies, and decision rights that outline detailed roles and responsibilities. I will not go into depth on these concepts in this chapter because I talk more about these important components in the following chapters, specifically Data Governance Planning, Organizational Framework, and Roles and Responsibilities.

What I will say is this is the most important starting point for any program. These four inputs define the "why," the "how," the "who," and the "what" details of the program. Without them, program participants have no course to follow and wind up adrift. Even if you have an operational program that is faltering, it is never too late to take a step back and formally define these four things.

Data Management

Data Management is a set of discreet capabilities that provides tactical execution of Data Governance policies and standards. Data Management encompasses those activities responsible for rigorously managing an organization's critical data assets on a day-to-day basis. Every organization I've worked with engages in Data Management activities. So does yours. You are creating, ingesting, sourcing, integrating, and consuming data. Someone in your organization has developed some data quality rules even if they are applied at the end of the data consumption line in a report. Someone has also developed a list of key attributes and their definitions, even if this basic information lives in a spreadsheet on a shared drive (or that person's head!). I argue that ongoing Data Management activities without the discipline and oversight that Data Governance provides continues the culture of a dependence on individual knowledge to truly understand and navigate the data landscape.

The different capabilities and recommended practices are described below. The recommended practices are included as a guide. When adopted, they can help alleviate some of the Data Management challenges an organization feels. Not all need to be adopted. You need to determine where your trouble areas are and then focus your efforts there.

Data Architecture

Data architecture represents the structure of an organization's logical and physical data assets. A solid data architecture requires the presence of a consistent logical and physical design for data that supports the overall data strategy and the organization's objectives. Standards, rules, and policies delineate how data is captured, stored, integrated, processed, and consumed throughout the enterprise. The standardization of policies and procedures prevents duplication of effort and reduces complexity caused by inconsistent design and implementation approaches. Most importantly, it is essential to document what you have in place. You cannot begin to make improvements if you do not understand the current environment.

Data models are foundational to a solid data architecture. I call this out specifically because they are typically challenges in most organizations I work with.

There are three types of data models that are foundational to understanding the data ecosystem: the conceptual, the logical, and the physical data models. Most organizations I work with do not create or maintain data models, especially the conceptual and logical models. The conceptual data model is a great tool as it provides the ability to understand the data environment from a business point of view. The logical model breaks the conceptual model subject areas into individual business entities, attributes, and their relationships. This makes it a great tool for graphically demonstrating how data requirements will meet defined business requirements. It can also show how a current model can support or needs to be extended for new requirements. The physical data model is the description of the physical design required for a specific database management system (e.g., SQL, Oracle, etc.). Oftentimes, the physical data model is created from reverse engineering the physical data structures as they exist. That would be equivalent to creating the design for a house after it has already been built. Other examples of data architecture artifacts include entity-relationship diagrams (ERD), data flows, policy documents, and system architecture diagrams.

Recommended practices for data architecture include:

- An Enterprise Data Architecture discipline formally exists that maintains a holistic view of the data using conceptual and logical data models.
- Data modeling and naming standards exist that ensure a uniform and consistent set of data models across the enterprise.
- Logical data modeling is a component of the business requirements process.
- Data requirements are clearly defined and aligned to the business requirements.
- Standards for data movement between various environments are developed and documented prior to development.
- A standard ETL (Extract, Transform, Load) tool is used that supports standardized ETL for integrated reporting and analytic platforms (e.g., Data Warehouse, Data Mart, Data Lake, etc.).
- ETL architecture and infrastructure are clearly defined and documented for hardware, databases, and software.

Data Administration

Data administration focuses on the maintenance of the physical data structures. It includes standards, retention and archiving, batch schedules and windows, and other topics of day-to-day data management and control. This discipline also ensures adequate capacity planning and monitoring methods are in place to support data needs. These administrative tasks are typically filled by an individual like a database administrator.

Recommended practices for data administration include:

- Physical data models exist and conform to data policies and standards (e.g., naming standards, standard data formats, standard domains, etc.).
- Policies and standards for data administration have been defined and documented.

- Data access is compliant with privacy and security policies.
- Data retention and archiving policies are in place and based on business and regulatory criteria.
- Processes for data archiving, disaster recovery, and return to normal business operations are well defined and in place.

Data Quality

Data quality directly impacts the level of trust users have in the data they use. It is the presence of processes and procedures for making data usable and reliable across the enterprise. Data quality is one of those areas that means different things to different people depending on when and how they interact with data. I will explore data quality more in Chapter 5, Common Starting Points.

Recommended practices for data quality include:

- Data quality process is part of Data Governance and is actively managed.
- Data quality processes are performed as close to the data source as possible.
- There is a closed loop data quality improvement process in place.
- Data profiling is completed prior to ETL specifications and ETL design (prior to data movement from source to target).
- Up-to-date, searchable documentation about data quality is available.
- Data quality service level agreements are in place that define data acceptance criteria.
- Data quality business rules are centralized.
- Self-service data and data movement are managed to ensure that multiple versions of "data quality" are not created.

Data Security

Data security is the presence of mechanisms to protect data from unauthorized use or distribution. The business organization is responsible for defining the levels of access required for various roles and groups, while the IT and security organizations are responsible for implementing the requirements in the system architecture. The Data Governance organization supports data security through aligning processes to established policies that may exist across different facets of the business. For example, Marketing efforts need to adhere to Legal's privacy policy.

Recommended practices for Data Security include:

- All data has been assigned a security data classification.
- Risk assessment is periodically performed to audit compliance with data security and access policies.
- Information Access policies and standards are in place for integrated data (data warehouse, master data management [MDM], data marts) and analytical data stores.
- Private cloud solutions have the same security, privacy, and compliance processes as internal data stores.

Metadata

Metadata is the presence of catalogs of business definitions, data lineage, and business rules for enterprise data. Like data quality, this is a typical starting point for most Data Governance programs because most organizations lack shared metadata processes. The concept will also be explored in greater detail in Chapter 5, Common Starting Points.

Recommended practices for Metadata include:

- Up-to-date, searchable documentation about business and technical metadata is integrated and available.
- There is a clearly identified process for the collection, review, approval, updating, and storage of metadata.
- Established roles exist across business and IT stakeholders to address business definitions of attributes and metrics, data origin, technical metadata, ownership, and validation responsibilities.

- Gathering and storing metadata begins with defining the terms and business rules discovered during business requirements.

Reference and Master Data

Reference data is presence and maturity of a repository of common data between systems and data used as lookup values for discrete data elements. Examples might be state or country codes or enterprise hierarchies such as product information.

Master data management (MDM) is the set of processes, technology, and data used to ensure that key business entities (e.g., customer, product, location) are defined and managed to ensure that they are a common data linkage point to integrate and aggregate data across the enterprise. It should be noted that Reference and Master Data Management cannot be successfully achieved without many of the other Data Management capabilities in a mature state, especially data architecture, metadata, and data quality.

Recommended practices for reference and master data include:

- MDM is aligned with the Enterprise Data Architecture and Data Strategy.
- MDM is managed as a program with a formal program manager accountable for MDM strategy and prioritization of enhancements and issues.
- People and processes are in place to ensure the completeness and accuracy of the reference and master data (e.g., data stewardship).
- MDM is centralized across lines of business whenever possible.
- MDM is integrated with all enterprise data, regardless of the size of the data environment (big or small).

Reporting and Analytics

Reporting and Analytics represents the effectiveness of systems supporting the creation of value from the data, the business intelligence, and analytics reporting capabilities within an organization. This is the area where many users interact with data assets and oftentimes question results. Because of this, it requires maturing disciplines in the areas of data architecture, metadata, and data quality.

Recommended practices for Reporting and Analytics include:

- Architecture and infrastructure are clearly defined and documented (for hardware, databases, and software) for analytic platforms (e.g., data warehouse, data marts).
- Business users have confidence in the accuracy, timeliness, and completeness of the data and reporting solution.
- Data integration of enterprise data is centralized.
- Data quality and standardization occur once and are not duplicated in other systems.
- Reporting and Analytics use standardized tools and follow a self-service model as much as feasible.

Data Life Cycle

The data life cycle is creating the awareness and implementation of systems and processes to manage data from its inception to its retirement. Most organizations I have worked with do not manage a complete data life cycle. Some even tell me they have policies in place, but they are not measured or complied with. There may also be conflicts between business objectives across departments. For example, Legal may want to purge records as soon as possible but Marketing may want to keep them for a longer duration to utilize in future programs.

Recommended practices for data life cycle include:

- Policies that pertain to data life cycle management exist, such as data creation, capture, data storage, data retention, data archiving, data destruction, and compliance and security.
- A tiered information storage model is used to reduce cost and increase efficiency in data storage and/or retrieval.
- A data lineage technology is used to paint a picture for both senior executives and users for how data flows through the enterprise.

Data Stewardship

Stewardship is the act of protecting a valuable resource and ensuring its health and sustainability. Data stewardship is no different. Data Stewards work to develop and protect information resources for the organization. Unlike other roles in a Data Governance program, Data Stewards play an integral part in the program because of their familiarity with core business processes and the impact of data on those processes and vice versa. In addition to their typical day jobs, they define data policies, monitor those policies, are responsible for data quality, help define business rules, measure compliance to rules, manage key business terms, and facilitate and drive communication between data stakeholders. Whew!

Because of their broad skill set, this is not a role you can typically fill by hiring from outside your organization. Data Stewards utilize their experience and knowledge of the organization in navigating and working well within the existing corporate culture. They bring to the table a level of organizational respect whether or not they are in a formal leadership role. The Data Steward role can exist as a business-focused role or as an IT-focused role. Regardless of where the position exists, individual Data Stewards not only have influence but also the wherewithal to improve the Data Management culture.

All that said, I have been in very few organizations where Data Stewardship exists as a formal role. And by formal role, I mean one where there are Data Stewardship activities explicitly called out in Human Resource job descriptions. Data Stewardship continues to be a side-of-the-desk job. In other words, it is oftentimes a courtesy and not a requirement. Chances of success in any Data Governance program are greatly increased when roles are formally defined and role expectations are formally measured against defined individual objectives. There is more on Data Stewardship models in Chapter 7, Organizational Framework.

Business Drivers

Business Drivers are the underlying reasons for taking on formal oversight of data assets. Many organizations still find it challenging to maintain an effective Data Governance program over time. An underlying reason is that the programs themselves are not aligned to overall business objectives, which are needed to drive a successful program.

Here are the most common drivers I see with my customers.

Customer Focus

Every organization wants to better understand their customers and how they interact with their products and services. If you are having a hard time with the word "customer," you can replace it with student if you are in education, citizen if you are in government, or patient or provider if you are in health care. In order to gain that single view focus of a customer, many organizations need the ability to reconcile records from multiple sources into one version of truth for a "golden" customer record. In order to do that, the customer must be defined. And what makes up that definition? The data! Data Governance can then provide oversight for maintaining that single customer record through common definitions, identified systems of trust, and data acceptance criteria.

Compliance Mandates

Compliance, whether internal or external, is a part of all of our lives. There are internal and external mandates that range from security to privacy to data sharing. Internal mandates might be generated in Legal (e.g., privacy policy). External mandates might begin with legislation (e.g., California Consumer Privacy Act). As such, every organization has some type of regulatory reporting that must be done, and it does not bode well for your organization if compliance reports must be re-stated because of some type of data quality or definitional issue. I have worked with several financial services organizations that were required to establish Data Governance because of an audit finding from a regulator. As soon as Data Governance was a "finding," the organizations were bound to establish a program and report progress or face penalties. Data Governance can support these mandates by providing the mechanism for measuring overall compliance to stated policies.

Mergers and Acquisitions

Mergers and acquisitions will always drive data needs. This can be at an enterprise level (a company acquiring or being acquired) or even at a line of business or department level (expanding, reducing, or reorganizing). There are many areas that need to be considered in the reconciliation of systems, data, definitions, processes, and people. If a mature Data Governance program exists in at least one of the entities, the time to reconcile can be substantially reduced. If not, it is a great time to begin formalizing processes for managing key business terms and the data that support them.

Decision Making

I had a Chief Financial Officer tell me once that they thought it was ridiculous that they had to wait until the 17th of any given month to get month-end reporting, in a good month. The reason was that there were so many processes and disjointed business rules that had been built over time that the smallest anomaly would delay the entire load and reconciliation process.

Users want access to quality data in a timely manner. They also want the ability to interact with the data in the format that works best for them, be it a report, dashboard, or dataset. Data Governance can provide the oversight for capabilities like metadata, data quality, and data integration that better enable the entire reporting and analytic life cycle, leveraging data to inform decision making.

Operational Efficiencies

Organizations can gain efficiencies by reducing costs, delivering faster, or making processes simpler. Here's a case in point. I worked with a large retailer, and they measured products at least seven times between their distribution center and the store shelf. Why? Because nobody could agree on height versus length versus depth. In addition, nobody trusted what the person in the process had done before them, much less their vendors who supplied that data when products were onboarded into the system. Another customer had so many duplicated datasets that each month, it was costing them millions to store and maintain. Data Governance can help in scenarios like these by identifying key terms and setting boundaries for when it is okay to create new or repetitive datasets.

Solutions

Solutions support Data Management capabilities through automation and repeatability of processes. Specific technology solutions can be embedded in the standards of Data Governance policies. In Table 3.1 we outline descriptions of the different capabilities outlined in the Data Management Framework and how the solutions can help.

Table 3.1 Data Management Capabilities.

Capability	Solutions provide the ability to. . .
Data Cleansing	Establish and enforce the rules and policies to ensure that data meets the business definitions and defined user acceptance criteria
Data Monitoring	Develop operational reporting on data quality detection and remediation processes
Business Intelligence	Deliver business insights through data consolidation, report creation, and analysis
Data Lineage	Manage and analyze data relationships and dependencies to understand where data comes from, how it is transformed, and where it is going; the visualization can support impact and root cause analysis
Data Visualization	Produce graphical representations of data in various forms, including dashboards and analytical structures/models
Data Profiling	Analyze existing data and potential new sources of data to determine its content to establish baselines, expose and measure quality or continuity issues; also provides users with insights into what data in a larger dataset might be useful
Data Integration	Combine data from multiple data sources to provide a consistent and unified view of the data; it includes the movement, processing, and management of that data for use by multiple systems, applications, tools, and end users
Metadata Repository	Acquire and store information about data, helping describe details about application data assets throughout the organization

(Continued)

Table 3.1 (Continued)

Capability	Solutions provide the ability to. . .
Machine Learning	Automate the process of building analytical models; part of artificial intelligence, it is based on the idea that systems can make decisions with minimal human intervention by learning from data and identifying patterns
Data Catalog	Create and maintain a searchable inventory of data assets including terms, definitions, business rules, and technical characteristics for data systems
Artificial Intelligence	Makes it possible for machines to learn from experience, adjust to new inputs, and perform human-like tasks
Master Data Management	Consolidate, standardize, and match common data elements, like customers or products, to achieve a more consistent view of these entities across the organization

Methods

Methods are how the overall Data Management/Data Governance program will be implemented and sustained. Organizational, process, and technology considerations are necessary to developing a holistic program. Methods will be discussed in depth in Chapter 12, Roadmap.

ALIGNING DATA GOVERNANCE AND DATA MANAGEMENT OUTCOMES

A simplistic way to think about an overall program is that Data Governance provides the oversight, monitoring, and communication of policies while Data Management provides the solutions and processes that support desired outcomes (i.e., compliance to said policies). Outcomes need to be aligned to program objectives (see Chapter 6, Data Governance Planning). Policies also need to be organizationally achievable at some point in the future. If they are not for reasons like lack of resources or misaligned authority, the Data Governance program will be deemed a failure.

The policy statements below are meant to be the rule that is broken down into procedures and standards. Chapter 13, Policies will include more detailed samples for metadata and data quality, but I thought

I would provide some policy statement examples here. Depending on your Data Governance focus, you may be able to use them as a starting point.

Data Architecture

Data architecture policies include statements about data models, data movement, data sharing, data integration, data standards, ETL standards, data access, and service level agreements. The outcomes of a policy might be standardized data movement, development of a data sharing architecture, and processes and tools for consistent data access. The benefits to policy compliance are things like reduced development time because of reusable components and trusted analytic sources.

Sample Policy Statement(s)
- A logical data model will be created and maintained to support business processes.
- An ETL architecture will be clearly defined and documented to support data integration activities.

Data Administration

Data administration policies are statements about day-to-day operations and control of physical data structures that might include data administration standards, data access, data retention, and the presence of a physical data model. Outcomes then would allow for standard approaches and a documented process for database administrators, compliance to overall privacy and security policies, and data retention and disaster recovery processes. It should be noted that the Data Governance organization will not typically write policies for data administration but may request that IT formally document their procedures to ensure consistent practices.

Sample Policy Statement(s)
- Access to data will be granted based on the IT and Legal data security policy.
- An up-to-date physical data model will be created and maintained.

Data Quality

Because data quality means so many things to so many people, a lot can be included in a data quality policy. Common focus for a policy includes statements for assessing, monitoring, reporting, and improving data quality. Outcomes can then mean data is profiled prior to development, there are automated data quality checks in place, data quality measures are collected and reported, and a remediation process is established. Data quality is discussed more in Chapter 5, Common Starting Points.

Sample Policy Statement(s)

- The Data Governance Office, in partnership with the appropriate business entities and support from IT, will proactively assess, monitor, report, and improve data quality. For the purposes of this policy, data quality is defined as the conformance of data to the business definitions and the business rules (business metadata). *(Note: This policy is reviewed in more detail in Chapter 13, Policies.)*

Data Security

Data security policies create the mechanisms to protect data from unauthorized use or distribution. Like data administration policies, the Data Governance organization might not necessarily own or develop the policies. For example, Legal may author and own the policy for data usage and protection. No matter where the policy is developed or owned, Data Governance can still provide compliance monitoring and communication. Data security policy content may include data classification, access, and sharing. Outcomes of the policy could mean formal adherence to enterprise policies, compliance with legal policies, and the ability to understand how data is being consumed and used in the organization.

Sample Policy Statement(s)

- Data that supports enterprise reporting and analytics will be classified and comply with organizational security policies.
- A risk assessment will be performed to audit and measure compliance with enterprise security and access policies.

Metadata

Like data quality, metadata is one of the most common starting points for a Data Governance program. Metadata policy contents include statements for common definitions, capturing and provisioning, and the minimum set of metadata to be captured. When implemented, outcomes will include a common location for documenting key business terms, measures, business rules, and hierarchies. Roles and responsibilities for the gathering, creating, maintaining, and sharing of metadata will also be defined. Metadata is more thoroughly explored in Chapter 5, Common Starting Points, and Chapter 13, Policies.

Sample Policy Statement(s)

■ Relevant business and technical metadata for data objects will be collected and published via a metadata repository. The metadata repository will be updated and maintained to ensure its relevancy. Metadata for the purpose of this policy is data that describes the business and technical characteristics of a data system, data source, data object, or data element. Metadata defines and gives value to a data asset. *(Note: This policy is reviewed in more detail in Chapter 13, Policies.)*

Reference and Master Data

Before talking about policy content for reference or master data, you should note that master data management is comprised of many of the other Data Management capabilities. Specifically, data architecture, metadata, and data quality. The content for the policy will include data integration, data standardization and correction, matching/merging records from various systems, data provisioning, and business rules. When mature, the outcome of the policy allows for a single, cleansed master record that is available for use across processes and systems. For example, a single customer record is built from attributes from multiple sources to utilize the "best," most up-to-date, or trusted customer information and provide insights for individualized marketing of products and services.

Sample Policy Statement(s)

▪ Customer data attributes will be identified, deduplicated, merged, and provisioned from the master data management hub in accordance with sanctioned standardization and business rules.

▪ Systems of record for master data entities will be identified and held accountable for defined data acceptance criteria.

Reporting and Analytics

Reporting and analytic platforms are a common place where people interact with data and therefore often identify problems with data. Policies in this area support the effectiveness of the platforms to enable value from the data. Like reference and master data, it is helpful to have other policies like data architecture, data quality, and metadata in place because they are key to a robust reporting and analytic platform. Components of the policy will include architecture, data integration, and tools. The outcomes then allow for an architecture that is aligned to the enterprise architecture, confidence in the data represented in reports, dashboards, or datasets, reduced data integration effort, and common tools that support a wide range of users.

Sample Policy Statement(s)

▪ Standard ETL processes and tools will be utilized for integration, cleansing, and load processes in the enterprise reporting environment.

▪ Data access and reporting tools will be provided to business stakeholders.

Data Life Cycle

Data life cycle policies will pertain to the management of data from its creation to its eventual destruction. Like data administration and data security, these policies might not be owned by the Data Governance organization but can provide the support for compliance reporting and communication. Policy content might include statements regarding data capture, storage, retention, archiving, and destruction. The outcome would be compliance to overall enterprise as well as potential legislative policies.

Sample Policy Statement(s)

- A tiered information storage model will be utilized to increase efficiency in data storage or retrieval.

MISALIGNING DATA GOVERNANCE AND DATA MANAGEMENT

A word of warning for your program. I have worked with a lot of customers who put too much hope for other challenges in Data Governance's lap. Data Governance and Data Management work together to ensure the best possible data outcomes. Neither are meant to be a replacement for IT Governance and project delivery methodology. Establishing a Data Governance policy and approving it are one step in the overall process. The final outcome of achieving compliance to the policy could mean several things that include organizational, process, or even a technology change. The technology changes are where I see the biggest challenge because, again, Data Governance and Data Management do not exist to solve how technology projects get done. Each has a different set of responsibilities to accomplish the business goal. This also means that just because there is a Data Governance policy, an IT project may have to be initiated to accomplish that business goal. Figure 3.2 shows technology delivery (at a high level) and where Data Governance and Data Management functions do not fit.

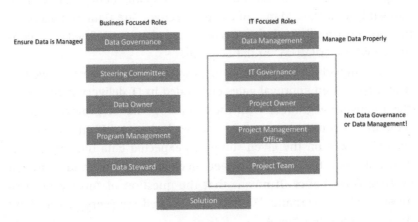

Figure 3.2 Data Governance/Data Management and IT Alignment.

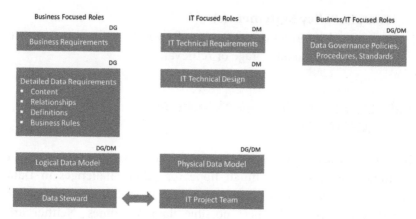

Figure 3.3 Data Governance/Data Management and IT Touchpoints.

There are definite touchpoints between Data Governance and IT project teams in solution delivery. Figure 3.3 depicts some of those touchpoints. How this applies to your organization is dependent on a number of factors including project delivery methodology, the scope of Data Governance, the overall IT strategy, and the data strategy (if it exists).

The boxes with "DG" show a definite alignment for Data Governance. Data Governance should be involved in business and data requirements. That involvement may be anything from approval to identifying the decision-making stakeholders. Data Management, denoted by a "DM," does not replace IT technical requirements and design but will be there in a supporting role to augment what needs to happen from a Data Management perspective. The Data Management function ensures that whatever is delivered aligns to defined policies as shown with a "DG/DM" in the diagram.

Data models, both logical and physical, need to be reviewed as well. I have seen approval gates embedded in IT delivery methodologies to ensure alignment with the Data Governance program. Lastly, Data Stewards must be involved and work closely with the IT Project Teams to focus on the given solution's expected data outcomes. This does not mean that every IT project needs to be vetted and approved by Data Governance. It means that the question of "do we need to involve Data Governance?" needs to be asked for every project (and the answer is often "yes").

DATA GOVERNANCE AND DATA MANAGEMENT SUMMARY

Data Governance provides the oversight, definition of roles and responsibilities, and communication while Data Management focuses on achieving the desired outcomes according to defined policies. I think it is easier to summarize as shown in Figure 3.4 which describes the core program functions with verbs. I call it Data Governance in Action.

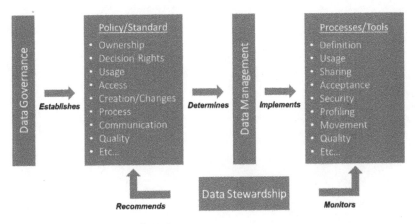

Figure 3.4 Data Governance in Action.

We start on the left with Data Governance, which **establishes** policies, procedures, and standards for everything from ownership to communication to definitions to quality. There is an "etc." at the bottom of the list because this list could include any number of things. That is going to depend on your unique set of challenges. Those policies, procedures, and standards then **determine** what Data Management is going to **implement** with the goal of becoming compliant with Data Governance policies. Those are typically processes or tools to automate or consolidate processes around metadata, data quality, data movement, or data usage. Again, the "etc." at the bottom of the list is there because the list needs to align to the list from Data Governance. Lastly, Data Stewardship **monitors** compliance to policies and uses their extensive knowledge and stakeholder network to **recommend** new policies or updates to existing ones.

CHAPTER **4**

Priorities

RESULTS YOU CAN EXPECT USING THE MOST COMMON APPROACHES TO PRIORITIZATION

Prioritization is hard. It is probably one of the most difficult things many of us do on a daily basis, whether in our work or personal lives. I've listed below the typical prioritization approaches I consistently see with customers.

The List

Everybody has one. Every department has one. Every organization has one. It could be a list of projects or issues that are ranked. It could also be a daily to-do list. It could also be a list of budget requests for the following year. This approach doesn't work because everybody has one and there is no consolidation across the various lists. It can be hard to reconcile lists across groups because criteria (what makes it on to the list, how the list is tackled, etc.) are not consistent.

Level

This approach to priorities is not systematic either; rather, it is based solely on the level of the person making the request. C-level and other high-level management folks tend to get their questions answered or issues addressed first. This is true even if they are merely pondering a thought instead of really asking for something to be done. This doesn't work because what might be important to the individual executive is not necessarily aligned with what is currently most important for the organization.

Volume

People tend to get louder as they get more frustrated. If somebody is talking loudly at you, it seems easier to answer their question if for no other reason than to make them go away so you can focus on your regular work.

This doesn't work because there is no focus and understanding that people are working on the most important thing for the organization.

Lunch

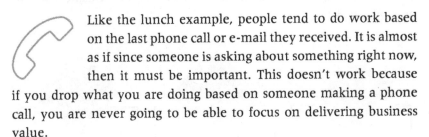 Remember how your lunch turned to work topics. And then your co-worker started asking how hard it might be to do something. Then you went back to your desk and started exploring. Then the afternoon was gone. As might be the next day. And the day after that. This doesn't work because if you are responding to requests based on the last lunch meeting you had, you haven't begun to ask if that question has value for the organization.

Communication

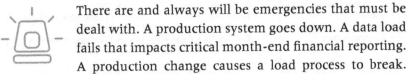 Like the lunch example, people tend to do work based on the last phone call or e-mail they received. It is almost as if since someone is asking about something right now, then it must be important. This doesn't work because if you drop what you are doing based on someone making a phone call, you are never going to be able to focus on delivering business value.

Emergency

There are and always will be emergencies that must be dealt with. A production system goes down. A data load fails that impacts critical month-end financial reporting. A production change causes a load process to break. Somebody needs to troubleshoot why .00002 of gender codes are blank. Wait. What? This approach doesn't work because not everything is an emergency that should stop the development of business value activities. All-hand-on-deck issues should be defined so people know when it is appropriate to stop work and focus on those issues instead of other work at hand.

A DISCIPLINED APPROACH TO PRIORITIES

Oftentimes, setting priorities is a combination of the scenarios I described above. The approach is undisciplined and leads to a chaotic environment. I suggest using an approach that considers business value and achievability. Of course, business value and achievability need to be defined before we can begin to talk about priorities. The idea here is to get everybody applying the same criteria to the things we want to prioritize in a way that is separate from where the issue arises (e.g., something from the issue or wish list(s), enterprise initiatives, standalone reporting and analytic needs, or even data enhancements).

Business Value

I like to use three basic inputs when thinking about business value. They are Strategic Alignment, Business Impact, and Business Readiness (Figure 4.1).

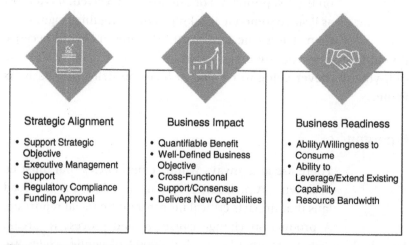

Figure 4.1 Business Value Definition.

Let's work up a definition for each of these items and then assign some values to a few hypothetical projects. Your definition might be different, but these questions are a great starting point.

Strategic Alignment

It is important for us to show that the things we are focused on matter to the business. The best way to do that is to align our priorities with that organization's strategic objectives. If we cannot align a so-called "priority" issue with a business objective, it is probably not the most important thing to focus on. In addition to aligning to a strategic objective, it is important to have executive level support. While it might be easy to somehow tie most everything to a defined strategic objective, having support from an executive (or better yet, a group of executives) demonstrates strategic alignment. Every organization has some level of regulatory and compliance work they have to do. Some are internal and some are mandated. This needs to be considered because again, there is some work we have to do. Lastly, if funding already exists, that demonstrates that somebody with funding authority believes it is in the best interest of the organization.

Here are the questions I start with:

- Does this support one or more of our organization's strategic objectives?
- Does this have the support of executive management?
- Is this a regulatory or compliance issue that we must address?
- Does this have funding approval?

Business Impact

When we deliver new functionality or solve a burning issue, we also want to be sure the change or fix has a positive impact on the business. The first thing that comes to mind is the bottom line. Generating revenue or reducing costs has positive impact. Another is having an understanding and the ability to define "why" something is important. In other words, having an end-goal in mind. A solution that supports or helps a business unit or the entire enterprise has more impact than a solution that is focused on an individual or a department. Lastly, delivering a new capability that solves a business problem positively impacts the business. I am not talking about changing a reporting tool and delivering the exact same reports. Something more impactful might be automating a manual or repetitive process.

Here are the questions I start with:

- Does this provide a quantifiable benefit?
- Is there a well-defined business objective?
- Is there cross-functional support?
- Does this deliver a new capability?

Business Readiness

Sometimes a project might be a great idea but for whatever reason, there is a lack of adoption. Therefore, it is important to ask some questions about the ability of the organization to adopt what we seek to implement. First off, the audience needs to be able and willing to consume or use whatever is delivered. I have seen a lot of IT projects with the strategy of "build it and they will come." More often than not, that thought process is not a strategy for enabling readiness. Another input into readiness would be the ability to leverage or extend an existing capability, whether that is a tool or a process. This is especially true in organizations where the culture is resistant to change. Lastly, users might want something or think the final product is a great idea, but if they do not have the time to properly devote to activities like requirements, reviews, and testing, the end result will more than likely be something they do not want and ultimately will not consume.

Here are the questions I start with:

- Is there an ability and willingness to consume what we deliver?
- Are we able to leverage or extend an existing capability?
- Do we have the bandwidth to support it?

Achievability

Achievability speaks to how "easy" something might be to complete. The three key inputs are Technical Complexity, Data Complexity, and Risk. As with Business Value, I offer you definitions and starting point questions for each category (Figure 4.2).

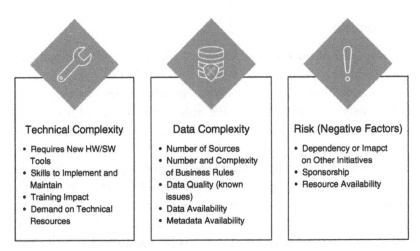

Technical Complexity

- Requires New HW/SW Tools
- Skills to Implement and Maintain
- Training Impact
- Demand on Technical Resources

Data Complexity

- Number of Sources
- Number and Complexity of Business Rules
- Data Quality (known issues)
- Data Availability
- Metadata Availability

Risk (Negative Factors)

- Dependency or Imapct on Other Initiatives
- Sponsorship
- Resource Availability

Figure 4.2 Achievability Definition.

Technical Complexity

You need to think about the ease of implementing a solution or correcting a problem. The first three questions are related and build on one another. If there is no need to install new hardware or implement a tool on top of what you are trying to do, the process will be easier. Along with that, having the skills to both implement and maintain the solution or fix makes it easier. If you do not need to implement new tools and already have the skill set, you more than likely do not need additional training. That will make it easier. Lastly, the technical teams always have full plates, so the availability of resources needs to be considered. If resources are readily available, that will be easier. If new resources need to be onboarded, the entire process becomes harder because of ramp-up time.

Here are the questions I start with:

- Can we achieve this with our existing technology?
- Do we have the skills to implement and maintain it?

- Do we need to get new training?
- Do we have the technical resources available?

Data Complexity

Because most of our focus is on data, I like to consider it separately from Technical Complexity. Data is an entirely different animal in getting something done so let's consider what types of things make dealing with the data easier. If we only need to deal with one data source as opposed to many, that makes our job easier. Hand-in-hand with the number of sources, our job is easier if we have access to the data and don't have to request and then create extracts. Business rules have the potential to create a lot of unknowns. Business rules are often not documented, buried in code, or may be applied at different points as data moves through the ecosystem. If data is loaded somewhere exactly as it is in its source, the data is less complex and therefore easier because there are no associated business rules. Business rules are often written to solve some underlying data quality issue. If we know about the issues, it makes dealing with data easier. Lastly, any data questions are more easily addressed if there is metadata available, up to and including full data lineage and source to target mapping that includes defined transformations or business rules.

Here are the questions I start with:

- Do we need to access many data sources?
- Is the data readily available?
- Will there be multiple complex business rules involved?
- Do we know about data quality issues?
- Is there metadata available?

Risk

While I've just talked about things that might make taking something on easier, there are also some factors that need to be considered that can make something harder. These are risk factors. Sometimes, in order to do something, we need something else to get done first. Or, if we do something there may be an impact to other initiatives or processes that will have to be addressed. Although either of these scenarios may be necessary, they will make it harder. I understand that executive sponsorship is an input into Strategic Alignment, but anything will be riskier, or more difficult, if that sponsorship does not exist. That is why you see it twice. The same can be said of both business and technical resource availability. The operative word there is "and." Both sets of resources are addressed individually, but if they are not available as a group then that will make whatever we are trying to accomplish harder.

Here are the questions I start with:

- Are there dependencies or impacts on other initiatives?
- Does executive sponsorship exist?
- Do we have the business and technical resources available?

UTILIZING THE MODEL

Now that we have defined what we mean by Business Value and Achievability, we can apply the series of what I call "Yes, Sort of, No" questions and begin getting results. I offer a few examples below from different scenarios. The first was a university that was building out a new reporting and analytic platform. This can be a great springboard for Data Governance because whatever data is being delivered to support reporting and analytics can fall under the umbrella of defined policies for managing data. The second is a retailer who wanted to understand where to focus Data Governance activities across different departments. Two different scenarios but you all went to school, and you all have shopped. The model was applied differently in both organizations but the questions we asked were still the same.

University – Formal Weighted Model

The university wanted to build out a new reporting and analytic platform. You can see their entire list of capabilities in Chapter 5, Common Starting Points.

Recall that Business Value = Strategic Alignment + Business Impact + Business Readiness and Achievability = Technical Complexity + Data Complexity + Risk.

With this university we used math and added one additional step to what I described above. We assigned a score and a weight to each of the inputs for business value and achievability. The score was straightforward for the "Yes/Sort of/No" questions in that each answer was assigned a numeric value: Yes = 7, Sort of = 4, and No = 1.

Next, we incorporated a weight. The idea is that one of the three inputs needs to be the most important consideration. The others may be lowest or somewhere in the middle. Table 4.1 shows the legend for the weight factor:

Table 4.1 Weight Factors.

Weight	Description	Weight Factor
Critical	Critical deciding factor	x10
High	Important deciding factor	x7
Medium	Consideration but not a deciding factor	x4
Low	Not a deciding factor	x1

This was the final determination for the university. They determined that from a Business Value perspective, Strategic Alignment was the most critical input so the spreadsheet weighted that input by a factor of 10. Data Complexity was rated as High, so those inputs were weighted by a factor of 7 while Business Readiness was assigned a weighted factor of 4. On the Achievability side of the equation, nothing was weighted as Critical. But Data Complexity and Risk were both deemed High, so the multiplier of 7 was applied while Technical Complexity was weighted at 4 with a Medium level of importance (Table 4.2).

Table 4.2 Assigned Weights.

Business Value	Weight	Achievability	Weight
Strategic Alignment	Critical	Technical Complexity	Medium
Business Impact	High	Data Complexity	High
Business Readiness	Medium	Risk (negative)	High

The next step is to answer the questions as I describe above. Before I can do that, let me provide a couple of the items on their prioritization list with a short description (Table 4.3).

Table 4.3 University Reporting and Analytic Capabilities.

Capability	Description
Student Progression	Provide an integrated view of leading and key performance indicators (KPI) that provide insight into student progression and academic progress across defined life cycle. Present views and drill-down by region, campus, modality, grad team, program, and so on. Progressively analyze, develop, and refine correlations and key indicators for predicting and forecasting student progression and outcomes.
Faculty Profiling & Segmentation	Understand and segment faculty based on demographics, academic qualifications, teaching preferences (including modality and program level), performance, and so on. Faculty profiling and segmentation will allow the university to optimize faculty utilization, increase satisfaction by aligning capabilities with ability to deliver, and identify hiring needs.
Employee Utilization	Provide insight and ongoing monitoring into employee utilization and trends to support staff forecasting, hiring, and budgeting. Trending and drill-downs must be available based on organizational hierarchy, roles, and regional/campus alignments.
Student Dashboard	Provide a consolidated view of a student's profile, demographics, academic history and standing, financial standing (including financial aid), and contacts/interactions with university faculty and staff. Provide operational insight and efficiency as well as supporting potential financial aid fraud research/detection.

There were more capabilities than listed, but remember, we asked the same questions of each of these capabilities, which would in turn become reporting and analytic capabilities as well as the data scope for Data Governance activities.

Now, here are the answers to each of the starting point "questions" for each input in a Yes/No format. The top row for each input is a summation of the individual answers into the overall Yes/Sort of/No format. I will admit that the summation is somewhat subjective, but we are using the same definition for each input. For example, if we answered Yes to the majority of the questions for Strategic Alignment, then the overall answer would be Yes. After a few iterations of this discussion, the detailed questions serve as a reminder about what we mean by the given input (Table 4.4).

Table 4.4 Detailed Yes/Sort Of/No Matrix.

	Category	Student Progression	Faculty Profiling & Segmentation	Employee Utilization	Student Dashboard
	Strategic Alignment	Yes	Sort of	No	No
	Does this support one or more of our organization's strategic objectives?	Yes	Yes	No	Yes
	Does this have the support of executive management?	Yes	Yes	No	No
	Is this a regulatory or compliance issue that we must address?	No	No	No	No
	Does this have funding approval?	Yes	No	No	No
	Business Impact	Sort of	Yes	Yes	No
	Does this provide a quantifiable benefit?	No	No	Yes	No
Business Value	Is there a well-defined business objective?	Yes	Yes	Yes	No
	Is there cross-functional support?	Yes	Yes	No	No
	Does this deliver a new capability?	No	Yes	Yes	Yes
	Business Readiness	Yes	Sort of	Sort of	Sort of
	Is there an ability and willingness to consume what we deliver?	Yes	Yes	Yes	Yes
	Are we able to leverage or extend an existing capability?	Yes	No	No	No
	Do we have the bandwidth to support it?	Yes	Yes	No	No

Table 4.4 (Continued)

	Category	Student Progression	Faculty Profiling & Segmentation	Employee Utilization	Student Dashboard
Achievability	Technical Achievability	Yes	Sort of	Yes	Sort of
	Can we achieve this with our existing technology?	Yes	Yes	Yes	Yes
	Do we have the skills to implement and maintain it?	Yes	No	Yes	No
	Do we need to get new training?	No	Yes	No	Yes
	Do we have the technical resources available?	Yes	No	No	No
	Data Achievability	Sort of	No	No	No
	Do we need to access many data sources?	Yes	Yes	No	Yes
	Is the data readily available?	No	No	No	No
	Will there be a lot of complex business rules involved?	Yes	Yes	No	Yes
	Do we know about data quality issues?	Yes	No	No	No
	Is there metadata available?	No	No	No	No
	Risk (negative)	No	Sort of	Sort of	No
	Are there dependencies or impacts on other initiatives?	No	Yes	Yes	Yes
	Does executive sponsorship exist?	Yes	Yes	No	No
	Do we have the business and technical resources available?	Yes	No	No	No

Let's simplify the table now with just the summary of the main inputs. Then we can talk about the math (Table 4.5).

Table 4.5 Prioritization Model Inputs.

	Category	Student Progression	Faculty Profiling & Segmentation	Employee Utilization	Student Dashboard
Business Value	Strategic Alignment	Yes	Sort of	No	No
	Business Impact	Sort of	Yes	Yes	No
	Business Readiness	Yes	Sort of	Sort of	Sort of
Achievability	Technical Achievability	Yes	Sort of	Yes	Sort of
	Data Achievability	Sort of	No	No	No
	Risk (negative)	No	Sort of	Sort of	No

Here is the formula I use: Category Score * Weight Factor. For example, the Student Progression capability has a Strategic Alignment score of Yes and Strategic Alignment is weighted as Critical so that math is 7 * 10 = 70. Remember that Risk makes things harder, not easier, so those numbers are negative (Table 4.6).

Table 4.6 Prioritization Weighted Scores.

	Category	Student Progression	Faculty Profiling & Segmentation	Employee Utilization	Student Dashboard
Business Value	Strategic Alignment	70	40	10	10
	Business Impact	28	49	49	7
	Business Readiness	28	16	16	16
	Business Value Total	126	105	75	33

Table 4.6 (*Continued*)

	Category	Student Progression	Faculty Profiling & Segmentation	Employee Utilization	Student Dashboard
Achievability	Technical Achievability	28	16	28	16
	Data Achievability	49	7	7	7
	Risk (negative factor)	–7	–28	–28	–7
	Achievability Total	70	–5	7	16

Now we have numbers for the Business Value and Achievability and can lay them out on a grid. Here is the final result for the four capabilities we just applied the weighted model to. The focus should be in the top right quadrant where you can expect the highest value and highest achievability (Figure 4.3).

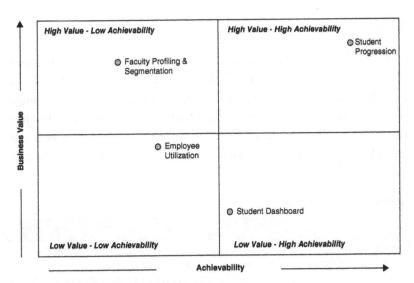

Figure 4.3 Sample Prioritization Model Output.

And now the entire set of priorities (Figure 4.4).

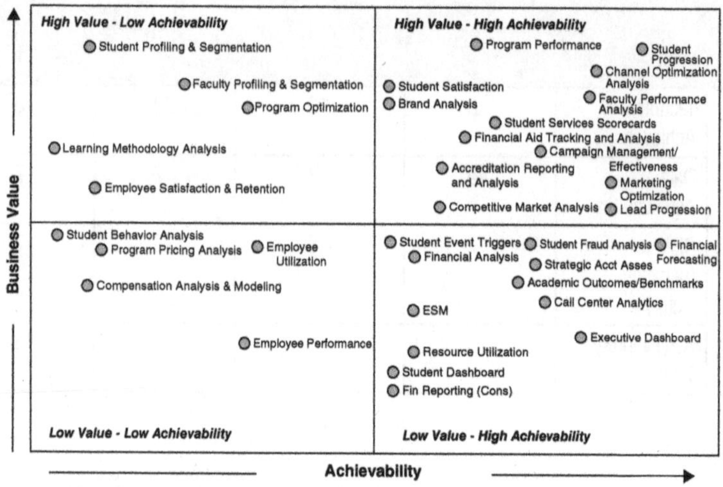

Figure 4.4 University Prioritization Output.

I will point out that Student Progression was the top priority for this program. It became the focus not only for development efforts but also for metadata and data quality activities that were defined through the Data Governance process.

Retailer – A Different Approach

Perhaps you do not want to create and maintain a spreadsheet or even feel like you need to double-check your math. You can still apply the disciplined approach as with the retailer example. Their data challenges were consolidated into four core functions that included Product, Customer (marketing function as well), Finance (reporting and analytics function as well), and Vendor. Here are a couple of examples of their challenges (Table 4.7).

Table 4.7 Retailer Challenges.

Capability	Description
Standardize Product Hierarchies/Categories	▪ Identify common set of product hierarchies required to support business processes across the enterprise. ▪ Eliminate duplicative or redundant hierarchies or categories. ▪ Determine business owners and procedures to maintain core hierarchies over time.

Table 4.7 (Continued)

Capability	Description
Privacy and Preferences	▪ Define policy and usage guidelines for customer data based on customer elections, purpose, and method by which customer data was acquired, accounting for published privacy policies.
Standardize Financial Metrics and Definition	▪ Identify enterprise KPI to monitor overall performance. ▪ Define standard definitions, data quality requirements, and certification methods.

We agreed on the criteria (the questions that I am not going to repeat). At an offsite meeting, each representative group had large Post-it Notes with the challenges that aligned to their area. The Vendor team went first and added their set of Post-it Notes to a large grid. Then the Finance folks got their turn, but the rule was they could move Post-it Notes that were already on the grid. By the time the Product team had their turn, the entire group was standing at the board discussing the different challenges. This created a cross-functional discussion, one that this organization had not experienced before. After several hours, they were able to come to agreement that Data Governance efforts should begin with the Product domain and focus on the standardization of a product hierarchy. Here is the final result of their exercise (Figure 4.5).

Figure 4.5 Retailer Priorities.

You may look at the grid and notice that there were two other items (Financial Metrics and Definitions and Privacy and Preferences) that were higher on the Business Value axis, and you would be right. Privacy and Preference was even higher from an Achievability perspective. The collective decision of all groups involved was that this retailer needed the ability to get their product catalog online and could not continue managing multiple product hierarchies in spreadsheets. This gave initial focus of the Data Governance program to defining a standard product hierarchy, and the data that supported core product attributes would fall under the Data Governance umbrella.

PRIORITIES SUMMARY

If your organization has a defined process for setting priorities, there is no need to reinvent the wheel. But if you are prioritizing inconsistently then I suggest adopting the method I defined above. It will give you a process for establishing your priorities and more importantly, focus for the Data Governance program. If you have already had the Panera Bread lunch and created that list of challenges, apply this process and focus first on the issue with the highest value and achievability.

CHAPTER **5**

Common Starting Points

RESULTS YOU CAN EXPECT WITH TOO MANY ENTRY POINTS

When organizations begin talking about Data Governance, it can quickly become a catch-all for any data-related issues. Trying to solve for every problem that may arise results in too many distractions and a lack of focus. Programs that take it all on at the beginning tend to fall apart not because of a willingness to improve but due to this lack of focus. Nothing is ever completed and stakeholders begin to wonder why they bother, and go back to their old workarounds.

BUILDING A DATA PORTFOLIO

You cannot begin Data Governance efforts with every data element in your data ecosystem in mind. So, how do you filter down to the most important data assets? A great place to start from that respect is with your reporting and analytic platform (regardless of whether you call it a Data Warehouse, Data Mart, Data Lake, Lakehouse, etc.) because that is where users interact with data and, coincidentally, find data issues.

The following is an example of a Business Data Portfolio. It is meant to represent the reporting and analytic capabilities required or desired by business stakeholders. The data subject areas at the top of the diagram logically reflect the data needed to support each of the capabilities with the understanding that data subject areas are used across multiple capabilities (Figure 5.1).

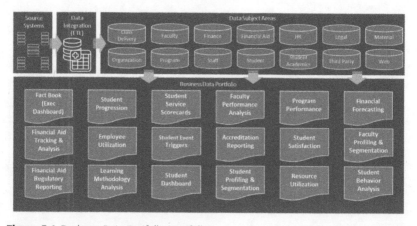

Figure 5.1 Business Data Portfolio (Portfolio).

The Portfolio has many benefits beyond Data Governance such as prioritizing data sources, having a clear understanding of current priorities, communicating what data is available for use, and promoting the re-use instead of re-creation of data assets. As far as the Data Governance program is concerned, the Portfolio sets the data scope for the program. In other words, the data that supports the different capabilities is subject to Data Governance oversight. If you have data scope for Data Governance activities, the program is much more manageable. That takes us to the two most common starting points for a program, metadata and data quality.

METADATA

Metadata is most often defined as "data about data" but that is overly simplistic. Metadata is information used to navigate through and understand the data landscape in an organization. For end users, it tells the story of how data was created, where it ended up, what happened to it along the way (e.g., business rules, transformations, etc.), and how it should be and not be used.

You can think of metadata by answering the most frequently asked questions about data:

- What data do we have?
- What is the definition?
- Where do I get it from?
- Where did it come from?
- When was it loaded?
- Has it been changed?
- Where can I use it?
- Who can see it?
- What am I allowed to call it?
- Who do I call if I have a question?

By answering these types of questions, actively managing metadata delivers value by helping to build data confidence, improving understanding of data relationships across systems, performing root cause analysis when data issues arise, and researching impact analysis for data changes. All of these things in turn improve overall data analysis and decision making.

Metadata Categories

Metadata can be separated into three primary categories. While each category supports a specific business or technical need, the entire set of metadata provides value to all metadata consumers. In other words, business users will find value in technical and operational metadata just as technical users find value in business metadata.

Business Metadata

The goal of business metadata is to provide answers to the above questions. There should be enough information that a user will understand what the data element means (most importantly), where it came from, and how it can be used. Data Stewards and business application subject matter experts or owners should be involved in defining metadata elements unique to their data subject area(s). Descriptions need to go beyond a regurgitation of a physical data structure. For example, if a field exists that is "first_name" to represent a customer's first name the description might be "Customer first name" and not "First name." The "customer" in the description denotes that we are not just talking about a first name but a customer's first name. Of course, the assumption exists that the term customer has also been defined.

Technical Metadata

Technical metadata describes characteristics of data such as physical location (host server, database server, physical schema, etc.), data types, any transformations applied, precision, and data lineage. IT staff uses it to design efficient databases, queries, and applications, and to reduce duplication of data. It also facilitates efficiency in requirements gathering for new systems as metadata will provide answers to many questions that come up during design and development.

- Technical metadata informs:
- Table name
- View name
- Column name
- Data type
- Data size
- Numeric precision
- Primary/Foreign key attributes
- Optionality
- Nullability

Operational Metadata

Operational metadata describes the characteristics of routine operations on data and related statistics. These include schedule and data job descriptions, status of data movement and transformation jobs, data read/update performance statistics, volume statistics, availability statistics, and backup and archival information. Daily information on data extraction, transformation, and loading (ETL) processes is important to understanding the current status of the data and its availability.

The metadata deployment stage must address two key goals: to provide requested metadata information directly to authorized information consumers and to provide the necessary metadata information that may be required to "metadata enable" data access tools (e.g., business reporting and analytical tool sets).

The removal of old metadata (retirement) maintains the usability of the repository by eliminating references to data that can no longer be used.

DATA QUALITY

If you hear any of these questions being asked in your organization, people are thinking about data quality.

- Why is my data giving me "conflicting information"?
- What data is "incorrect"?
- Why am I getting my data so "late"?
- Why are there so many "duplicates"?
- Why do I have "missing" data?
- Is my data "complete"?
- Does my data align with "enterprise standards"?

These questions are dependent on how and when users interact with data. A report consumer might care about "conflicting information" while a developer might care about "enterprise standards", while a data analyst or scientist might care about "missing data".

So, how should one approach data quality? The first step is to understand the different personas and what they care about. The second is adopt a definition for data quality. Here it is: *Data quality is the conformance of data to the business definitions and the business rules.* In other words, alignment to the metadata. It should be noted that data without business metadata can have no defined quality. Assertions about poor data quality are anecdotal at best.

Data quality can be broken down into four key categories as described below (Table 5.1).

Table 5.1 Data Quality Dimensions.

Data Quality Dimension	Description
Business Definition	The business definition provides context to the data and describes what it means in business terms.
Data Element	Defined quality for individual data elements; think about the columns in a table.
Data Record	Defined quality for an entire record; think about the rows in a table.
Data Movement	Defines quality as data moves through the data ecosystem.

Let's explore each of these categories in more detail and work through examples.

Business Definition

The quality of a business definition sets context for the data. If the definition, any business rules applied, valid content, intended business purpose, or current data quality are unclear, you cannot take the next logical step, which is measuring or improving the quality of the data. Consider the following record (Table 5.2).

Table 5.2 Record with No Context.

1985	BROWN	EMMETT	LATHROP	9165554385	2/29/1920	1640	RIVERSDE	HILL VALLEY	CA	95420	100	200

At first glance, it more than likely reflects some type of customer record. But how can you be sure? "1985" could be a year or some type of identifier. "2/29/1920" looks to be some type of date. "RIVERSIDE" could be a street or a city. "100" and "200" mean nothing as they are just numbers.

Now let's add some context to the data elements. Even something as simple as column headers begins to add definition to the fields. Of course, simply adding headers is not meant to take the place of more detailed metadata described in the section above (Table 5.3).

Table 5.3 Record with Better Context.

CUST_ID	LAST	FIRST	MID	PHONE	DOB	ST_NO	STREET	CITY	STATE	ZIP	CHK_ID	SVG_ID
1985	BROWN	EMMETT	LATHROP	9165554385	2/29/1920	1640	RIVERSDE	HILL VALLEY	CA	95420	100	200

Data Element

Data element quality is the measurement of conformity of the data to the metadata. This includes the following (Table 5.4).

Table 5.4 Data Element Quality.

Data Element	Description
Domain integrity	Data type of field ▪ Does a date field contain a date?

(Continued)

Table 5.4 (Continued)

Data Element	Description
Correct contextual value	Business metadata and business rule validation ▪ Can the field be validated against the business definition?
Cross-field validation	Business rules that relate two or more fields ▪ Does this city belong with this state? ▪ Do the zip code and city align?
Format consistency	Correct format of a field ▪ Does the date align to data standards? (e.g., MM/DD/YYYY)

Here are some records to consider with the measurements described above (Table 5.5).

Table 5.5 Records for Data Element Quality.

CUST_ID	LAST	FIRST	MID	PHONE	DOB	ST_NO	STREET	CITY	STATE	ZIP	CHK_ID	SVG_ID
765	BANKS	GEORGE	G	867-5309	8/14/1945	24	MAPLE	SAN MARINO	CA	91106	300	785
6453	SEAVER	CAROL	ANNE	631-421-4701	5/16/1969	15	ROBIN HOOD	HUNTINGTON	NY	11711	552	561
22	HOLMES	SHERLOCK	SCOTT	+44 20 7231 1212	4/4/1965	221B	BAKER	LONDON	UK	NW1 6XE	505	300

Here are some observations about the sample data (Table 5.6).

Table 5.6 Data Element Quality Dataset Notes.

Data Element	Description	Notes About the Dataset
Domain integrity	Data type of field ▪ Does a date field contain a date?	▪ The DOB fields all contain dates.
Correct contextual value	Business metadata and business rule validation ▪ Can the field be validated against the business definition?	It depends on the customer definition. If the definition is "any U.S.-based person with a checking or savings account" then Sherlock Holmes cannot be a customer because his address is in the U.K.
Cross-field validation	Business rules that relate two or more fields ▪ Does this city belong with this state? ▪ Do the zip code and city align?	We would need to know that San Marino is in CA and that the correct zip code is 91106.

Table 5.6 (Continued)

Data Element	Description	Notes About the Dataset
Format consistency	Correct format of a field • Does the date align to data standards? (e.g., MM/DD/YYYY)	George Banks's phone number is missing three digits, either the area code or the first three of the phone number.

Data Record

Data record quality is the measurement of the validity of an entire record. This includes the following (Table 5.7).

Table 5.7 Data Record Quality.

Data Record	Description
Completeness	Fields required to be a complete record • Is the record complete? • What fields are required?
Accuracy	Business metadata and business rule validation • Is the data accurate for the record?
Duplication	Duplicate records • Is there a duplicate record? • Should the records be merged?
Validation	Cross-table record validation • Are there records that should not exist? • Are there missing records?

Here is some sample data. In order to determine the quality of an entire record, you first need to understand the definition of a complete record. After that, you can explore data accuracy for the record and even look for duplicate records and cross-table record validation (Table 5.8).

Table 5.8 Records for Data Record Quality.

CUST_ID	LAST	FIRST	MID	PHONE	DOB	ST_NO	STREET	CITY	STATE	ZIP	CHK_ID	SVG_ID
27	WAYNE	BRUCE	THOMAS	713-896-0300	2/19/1963	1007	MOUNTAIN	GOTHAM	NY	60035	1700	1701
99	MAN	BAT		#BATSIGNAL	2/19/1963	1007	MOUNTAIN	GOTHAM	NY	60035	1700	1701
5653		JOKER			15/35/0000					99999	3750	

Here are some observations about the dataset (Table 5.9).

Table 5.9 Data Record Quality Dataset Notes.

Data Element	Description	Notes About the Dataset
Completeness	Fields required to be a complete record ▪ Is the record complete? ▪ What fields are required?	▪ A complete record needs to be defined. If the business definition of a customer is a person with a checking account, the JOKER would be a complete record. However, if the definition is a person with an account that can be contacted, the JOKER would not meet that criterion.
Accuracy	Business metadata and business rule validation ▪ Is the data accurate for the record?	Phone numbers do not usually begin with a '#'. We would expect to see numbers in this field. If a valid phone number is required, this record would be invalid. Also, the JOKER's birth date makes no sense. If it is determined that this is a complete record, name, address, and birth date info would need to be addressed.
Duplication	Duplicate records ▪ Is there a duplicate record? ▪ Should the records be merged?	BRUCE WAYNE and BAT MAN have different IDs but share the same birthdate, address, and checking account. This should beg the question, "Is Bruce Wayne Batman?"
Validation	Cross-table record validation ▪ Are there records that should not exist? ▪ Are there missing records?	One would expect to see a checking account record for BRUCE WAYNE and BAT MAN. One would also not expect to see a savings account for the JOKER. If either of these are not the case, the data will need to be explored.

Data Movement

From the time data is created, it moves through the data ecosystem. This includes data entering and exiting the organization, source system to source system, source system to reporting and analytic platforms, platform to a user's desktop, and so on. As the data makes its journey, it can be augmented or transformed. It is important to add checks along the way, similar to how an assembly line works. There are also inspections along the way or gates that have to be passed in order to move to the next step. Documenting the data quality checks (especially data element and data record) as data moves through each step in its journey ensures a level of trust for the end user in the resulting report, dashboard, or dataset.

DATA PROFILING

The examples above are meant to be simple. By only looking at one to three records, we were able to start thinking about data quality with a quick glance at the data. That is not the reality in most organizations. We need to make the same determinations but over thousands of records and do it as quickly as possible. This is where data profiling enters the picture.

Data profiling is the analysis of the data in a structured and organized manner with the goal of defining its level of quality, identifying specific data quality issues, and helping determine how to resolve those issues. Data profiling is important for every organization. It dramatically reduces the cost and time to complete data projects because data issues are proactively found and business rules for the data are identified before code/ETL is written. Data profiling is used to examine columns, rows, and multi-table relationships.

The different types of results from data profiling include those in Table 5.10.

Table 5.10 Data Profiling Analysis Components.

Column Profiling Analysis Components	Description
Column Analysis	Provides column domain results and statistics of the analysis performed on each individual column in the dataset including total and percentage of null and non-null fields, min/max values, and data types/lengths.
Frequency Distribution Analysis	Provides aggregated results on the number of occurrences a value may have for an individual column.
Pattern Frequency Analysis	Provides aggregated results of the distinct patterns of the data values within each column.
Data Validation	Verifies that data in your table or dataset matches its appropriate description.
Referential Integrity	Verifies that when one table has references to rows in another table, those rows exist in the other table.

The end result of profiling data provides insight into the data and identifies data quality issues including:

- Data errors
- Inconsistencies
- Data patterns and frequencies of errors
- Accuracy and validity of the data
- Errors based on data dependencies (i.e., column and table dependencies)
- Inaccurate or missing metadata
- Reliable data sources

In addition, having better insights into data allows for the establishment of data quality baselines, designing business rules, and setting scope for Data Governance program efforts.

COMMON STARTING POINTS SUMMARY

Starting something like Data Governance can be an overwhelming task. I recommend breaking down the problem. I will help you with priorities in Chapter 6, Data Governance Planning. If you can create something like a Portfolio, you will have the data scope. From there, you can think about the types of metadata important to both business and IT stakeholders, so they understand what data is available, where to find it, what to call it, what has been done to it, and how to use or not use it. From there, establishing a data quality baseline will help in development of data quality processes. Think about data quality in terms of business definition (where data quality and metadata intersect), data element, data record, and data movement quality. There are samples of a metadata and data quality policy in Chapter 13, 'Policies'.

For you pop culture nerds out there who thought some of the records might look familiar, you were right. Emmett Brown is from *Back to the Future*, George Banks is *Father of the Bride*, and Carol Seaver is from *Growing Pains*. Sherlock Holmes, Bruce Wayne/Batman, and the Joker need no explanation.

CHAPTER 6

Data Governance Planning

RESULTS YOU CAN EXPECT WITHOUT PLANNING

With Data Governance we often ask people to change how they do their jobs or even take on new roles in support of the program. In order to get buy-in for participation and from leadership, people need to understand why the organization is taking on Data Governance. If you cannot explain the why, people usually respond with "why bother then?" Or people take on a role and have no idea what they are supposed to do. Lastly, there is no way to define a program because there are no defined objectives.

DEFINING OBJECTIVES

Having program scope allows you to define program objectives. They are truly the cornerstone of the program and serve several purposes. The first is the communication mechanism for senior leadership. We need their buy-in and sponsorship in order to sustain the program. Because of that, we need to tell them why it is important and what we are trying to achieve. The second is that objectives drive activities and decisions that ultimately drive roles and responsibilities for program participants. Lastly, objectives determine how we will measure program outcomes.

I have worked with a lot of customers who have been part of a derailed Data Governance program. My first question to them is "have you defined objectives?" More often than not, the answer is no. Or sort of. My first recommendation then becomes to take a step back and write down what is important to achieve. It is never too late to define measurable objectives for their program. I have also worked with customers who can talk about what they want to accomplish but have not taken the time to write those things down. My recommendation is to formalize them into their program objectives.

Remember the list you created during the Panera Bread lunch? Here are some examples of themes from that infamous Data Governance kick-off. These are examples that I have purposely kept broad. Your list may be very detailed (e.g., my daily sales report never matches the one Joe produces) but the approach to breaking down the list to create objectives is the same.

- It costs too much to make a simple change to a table or report.
- We have to go to IT every time we want a new filter on our reports.
- It's hard to pull data from the application and move to Excel.
- Everybody has a different definition of a customer (or "insert your own data point here").
- We don't know what to do when the data in our reports is wrong.
- Data Governance hasn't worked in the past, so it probably won't this time around either.
- There's no telling what happens to data between the source system and the final report.
- We have no idea what data is available to us for use.
- If we fix data in the data warehouse, it just gets overridden on the next load – the source systems send bad data.
- Every developer in IT approaches managing the data differently.

If there is a set of statements, the next question is "what do you do about it?" In order to solve the problem, you first need to understand why there is an issue to begin with. I recommend taking the statements and breaking down the "why." It might look something like this (Table 6.1).

Table 6.1 "The List" and Potential Root Causes.

The List	Root Cause(s)
It costs too much to make a simple change to a table or report	- The number of hours from IT are too high - Developers do not know the impacts of changes - What little documentation that exists is out of date
We have to go to IT every time we want a new filter on our reports	- It takes a long time because IT's backlog is so long - There is no process for setting priorities - It is way faster and easier to download data to Excel - Users only have access to desktop applications like Excel or Access

(Continued)

Table 6.1 (*Continued*)

The List	Root Cause(s)
It's hard to pull data from all the applications and move to Excel	▪ Every application we use has a different report interface ▪ There is no easy way to know how to tie data together from different applications ▪ The process to download data from applications, move to Excel, and then integrate is manual and time consuming ▪ The same types of processes are being applied in multiple departments, yet they yield different results
Everybody has a different definition of a customer (or "insert your own data point here")	▪ There is little or no communication across departments ▪ Different functions need to think about customers differently ▪ Filters are applied inconsistently regarding the customer ▪ Reports that contain customer metrics do not match
We don't know what to do when the data in our reports is wrong	▪ There is no defined process for data issues or questions ▪ The help desk does not know enough about the data to troubleshoot
Data Governance hasn't worked in the past, so it probably won't this time around either	▪ Data Governance was a courtesy, not a requirement ▪ Too many people had too many ideas about how to get started ▪ People were assigned roles with no authority to make decisions
There's no telling what happens to data between the source system and the final report	▪ Source-to-target mappings are not complete ▪ Data lineage is not readily available ▪ Business rules are applied inconsistently
We have no idea what data is available to us for use	▪ Data sources are not defined ▪ Metadata process is not defined ▪ There are no defined roles for metadata creation, updates, or provisioning ▪ There is no formal training to understand what data to use or where to find it ▪ There is no identified individual data point of contact to support questions
If we fix data in the data warehouse, it just gets overridden on the next load – the source systems send bad data	▪ There is no data quality process in place ▪ Data acceptance criteria has not been established ▪ Data quality roles have not been defined ▪ Business metadata has not been defined so there is no baseline against which to measure data quality
Fields in different tables are called different things (e.g., "customer_name," "name," "col001")	▪ Data standards do not exist ▪ Developers are not aware of naming conventions ▪ There is no data architecture strategy in place to inform naming standards

If we can understand the root cause of an issue, then we change the issue into an objective for our program. Here are potential objectives for the issues identified above. There may be others based on the "why." The idea here is that each of the potential objectives begin with a verb and can be assigned a measurement (Table 6.2).

Table 6.2 Turning Root Causes into Objectives.

The List/Root Cause(s)	Potential Objective
• It costs too much to make a simple change to a table or report • The number of hours from IT are too high • Developers do not know the impacts of changes • What little documentation that exists is out of date	Reduce overall implementation and data remediation efforts/cost
• We have to go to IT every time we want a new filter on our reports • It takes a long time because IT's backlog is so long • There is no process for setting priorities • It is way faster and easier to download data to Excel • Users only have access to desktop applications like Excel or Access	Increase the ability to perform self-serve reporting and analytics
• It's hard to pull data from all the applications and move to Excel • Every application we use has a different report interface • There is no easy way to know how to tie data together from different applications • The process to download data from applications, move to Excel, and then integrate is manual and time consuming • The same types of processes are being applied in multiple departments, yet they yield different results	Increase the ability to integrate data, decreasing siloed approaches
• Everybody has a different definition of a customer (or "insert your own data point here") • There is little or no communication across departments • Different functions need to think about customers differently • Filters are applied inconsistently regarding the customer • Reports that contain customer metrics do not match	Establish standard definitions for key entities' data to promote consistency and accuracy
• We don't know what to do when the data in our reports is wrong • There is no defined process for data issues or questions • The help desk does not know enough about the data to troubleshoot	Provide a consistent process to address data issues across the Department

(Continued)

Table 6.2 *(Continued)*

The List/Root Cause(s)	Potential Objective
▪ Data Governance hasn't worked in the past, so it probably won't this time around either ▪ Data Governance was a courtesy, not a requirement ▪ Too many people had too many ideas about how to get started ▪ People were assigned roles with no authority to make decisions	Communicate the activities and importance of Data Governance
▪ There's no telling what happens to data between the source system and the final report ▪ Source-to-target mappings are not complete ▪ Data lineage is not readily available ▪ Business rules are applied inconsistently	Improve efficiency, visibility, and transparency in data processes
▪ We have no idea what data is available to us for use ▪ Data sources are not defined ▪ Metadata process is not defined ▪ There are no defined roles for metadata creation, updates, or provisioning ▪ There is no established data onboarding training available ▪ There is no defined data point of contact to support questions	Enhance the ability to identify data needed for decision making
▪ If we fix data in the data warehouse, it just gets overridden on the next load – the source systems send bad data ▪ There is no data quality process in place ▪ Data acceptance criteria has not been established ▪ Data quality roles have not been defined ▪ Business metadata has not been defined so there is no baseline against which to measure data quality	Communicate issues and decisions that impact creators and users of the data
▪ Fields in different tables are called different things (e.g., "customer_name," "name," "col001") ▪ Data standards do not exist ▪ Developers are not aware of naming conventions ▪ There is no data architecture strategy in place to inform naming standards	Establish standard repeatable processes that enable consistent data delivery

Our Objectives

In addition to the sample objectives above, here are some examples you might use as a starting point for your program along with why my customers thought these would work for them. Some are similar to the potential objectives listed above, some are different. Also remember the key themes from Chapter 1, Introduction? I have aligned the sample objectives to those themes. You will see these objectives again in later chapters when we talk about roles and responsibilities and program measurement (Table 6.3).

Table 6.3 Sample Objectives.

Key Theme	Sample Objective	Comments
Data Ownership, Reliance on Individual Knowledge	Establish an organizational framework with clear roles and responsibilities that enables sustainable execution across multiple domains	Every customer I have worked with has adopted some form of this objective and I recommend you do so as well. Establishing Data Governance requires change in the organization. That change, represented in program activities and participation, needs to be measured just as much as adherence to established policies.
Data Integration, Data Architecture	Ensure core data domains are integrated into single versions to support reporting/ analytic needs across departments	This customer had 72,000 MS Access Databases on their network that contained the same or similar customer and product data. Not only did that pose a security risk due to customer information being readily available, but it was also a nightmare trying to perform impact analysis because many of those databases were central to core business processes.
Trust in Data	Increase the overall trust in data through implementation of a data quality process	Every customer I have worked with wants to improve overall data quality, so some form of this objective is on every list of objectives. Remember the words are important. This particular customer had multiple sets of tools and dedicated data quality analysts; however, no process had been defined so individual processes were applied across multiple subject areas. Data quality processes need to be consistent, and Data Governance can provide the oversight for that consistency.

(Continued)

Table 6.3 (Continued)

Key Theme	Sample Objective	Comments
Metadata, Trust in Data	Establish a metadata process to ensure business rules, policies, documents, and updates are accessible and searchable across departments	I have already talked about the need for metadata in order for data quality to be truly measured. Most customers I work with do not have a metadata process beyond someone managing definitions and maybe source-to-target mappings for key fields they use. Oftentimes, it is not shared beyond users who may ask a question. In this organization, the Chief Operating Officer was tired of each department reporting they were meeting or exceeding up-time and processing metrics but overall (the collective of all the departments) metrics were on a downward trajectory. That is because each department was using their own set of definitions and rules. We established a centralized metadata process to produce common definitions and business rules across each of the departments.
Reliance on Individual Knowledge	Generate awareness around the use of the data, its value, and the need for governance	Like measuring establishment of the program, it is important to be able to communicate the progress of the program. I talk with customers a lot about awareness of data assets and the value it can provide. That is achieved through communication and training. Once users become used to the idea of valuable data, they crave more of it. And they want to trust it. That is the hook for Data Governance oversight.
Data Ownership Reliance on Individual Knowledge	Assign clear authority and accountability for data assets	It is not good enough to rely on individuals to answer questions about data. It is also not good enough for developers to make decisions about how data is represented in a final report or dataset. There needs to be an assigned individual (or group of individuals) who are empowered to make those decisions. This customer wrote their objective in response to an aging workforce with too much knowledge locked away in their heads or embedded in thousands of lines of code. They decided it was time to ensure there was a defined point of decision making for key data elements.

Table 6.3 (*Continued*)

Key Theme	Sample Objective	Comments
Metadata, Trust in Data	Maintain a consistent definition of the data and its business rules	This objective is similar to the establishment of a metadata process. The difference is this customer had a process but was not following it. They identified "high-impact" data elements and defined exactly what metadata would be captured for those data elements.
Data Architecture, Trust in Data	Eliminate redundant or conflicting business processes and practices	This organization physically measured products at least seven times between the distribution center and the store shelf. There are two reasons for this. The first was that there was no agreement on product dimensions (height versus width versus depth) and how to capture them, so as products moved through the life cycle, each department re-measured because there was a lack of trust in what information was being provided. The second was that the overall architecture did not provide a means for moving trusted data through the product data ecosystem. I have had many other customers adopt this objective for differing reasons like re-work and duplicate data. You may see a need in your organization as well.

DEFINING GUIDING PRINCIPLES

Guiding principles are statements of purpose that guide behavior. They are the set of common philosophies intended to direct a program or organization irrespective of day-to-day changes. Ideally, they will reflect the organization's values and goals. Their purpose is to serve as a philosophical touchstone for questions or dilemmas during Data Governance deployment. Unlike program objectives, they are not measured against but really set guardrails for a program. In other words, they are statements about "how" the program might be executed. A good set of guiding principles can also alleviate anxiety from program stakeholders, whether or not they are directly involved in day-to-day program operations.

I do not use the same type of process I described above to get to objectives because guiding principles have to resonate with the organization's culture. They need to be reflective of the organization's vision, mission, and core values. Here are some good examples to use as a starting point for your program along with some comments about why I think they are good (Table 6.4).

Table 6.4 Sample Guiding Principles.

Sample Guiding Principle	Comments
Data Governance will be facilitated centrally, executed "locally"	You use the term Data Governance and people tend to believe that yet another bureaucratic process is being added to make their jobs harder. This statement implies that decision making will be as close to the data as possible but there will be common execution processes. The central facilitation also tells stakeholders that someone else will handle the administrative aspects of Data Governance.
Clear authority and stewardship will be established for shared data	There will be an impact to program participants' roles, whether it is creating new responsibilities or formalizing tasks people are already doing. This statement serves two purposes. The first is making it clear that shared data will have oversight through stewardship. The second is that the people who are asked to be stewards will have the authority to make the decisions they are being asked to make.
Shared data shall be subject to defined information policies and standards	Sometimes it is easier to create a new table and manipulate some of the fields to meet a requirement. Sometimes it is easer to add a new column and make up a name for it. Other times, new logic can be applied to an existing field. It might be easier at that point in time, but not over the long haul. Developers can change the definition of a "customer" by adding fields or changing filters that can impact numerous downstream systems. Changes like this, for data that is shared by many, need to be vetted so there is approval and communication. This statement does just that and serves as a reminder that if there are policies in place for identified data, they need to be followed.
Investment will be made in people and training to effectively govern and manage data	I have heard many tales of woe of customers who are part of Data Governance and have no idea what it means, nor do they have tools beyond the Microsoft suite. This statement clearly says that participants in Data Governance will be provided training to understand their role. It also goes on to say that tools, if required, will be provided (along with the requisite tool training).

Table 6.4 (Continued)

Sample Guiding Principle	Comments
Collaboration, communication, and transparency will be embraced across departments	People feel a sense of ownership and responsibility over the data assets they use on a regular basis. People fear others taking the data they perceive to be theirs and doing something to it that might come back to haunt them. That could be anything from adding an additional filter to change the outcome to calling it something different to publishing the data externally. This mindset makes it difficult for data sharing across departments or divisions to be part of the data culture. In other words, departmental silos are created. This guiding principle sets the expectation that data will be shared across departments, but also that there will be communication.
Program objectives and outcomes will be monitored, measured, and reported	Measurement of the Data Governance program is important. Reporting status, successes, and challenges is important. This statement guarantees that there will be program oversight and the stated objectives will be monitored and measured. Program participants may need to provide updates to the program management function, so this guiding principle can serve as a reminder that information may need to be provided when asked.
Data architecture will be an enterprise-wide endeavor	Oftentimes data standards are based on point solutions. In other words, applications developed are created to solve a very specific problem or use case. Architecture decisions are made to deliver these solutions one at a time and usually the data is considered as an afterthought. That includes things like integration, storing, provisioning, using, and defining. This statement sets the groundwork that data architecture decisions will have an enterprise lens. This can be a reminder that there might be certain "gates" development projects need to pass through before implementation.
Data for reporting and analytics will originate from the source systems	Data originates somewhere. Then it moves. Sometimes it changes as it is moved. Then the new data gets used as a source. Then it moves again. Sometimes it changes as it is moved. Repeat this cycle any number of times and the problem gets worse. This statement draws a line in the sand that any data on a reporting and analytic platform will have come from a source system and not a copy of a copy of a copy of source system data.
Data Governance practices will be embedded within business and IT processes	Typically, there are processes for managing application projects. Data Governance processes need to be a part of those processes so the tasks and decision points are not overlooked or forgotten, which, in turn, continues the challenges we are trying to address. This guiding principle reminds people there is a Data Governance organization that needs to be connected to projects with data impacts.

(Continued)

Table 6.4 (Continued)

Sample Guiding Principle	Comments
We will align to industry standards whenever possible	All industry verticals have some type of industry-specific standards. A lot of organizations create their own because many of their applications are in-house. A great example of a customer I worked with was a retailer whose product hierarchy aligned to their organizational structure for merchants. In other words, products rolled up to whatever department the merchandising lead was in. That meant that "bottled water" aligned to "rough plumbing," making it difficult to manage things like inventory, store operations, and reporting. This guiding principle made the point that industry standards (e.g., product hierarchy) would be considered first and there would be deviations only if there was a business need.
Adoption and participation are mandatory	Many of my customers cite lack of participation in Data Governance as a challenge, especially over the long haul. Many program participants and stakeholders impacted by Data Governance decisions feel program participation is a courtesy and not a requirement. If a project is getting behind, the last thing someone needs to do is ask permission of a Data Governance organization to make some type of change. They just do it to get the job done. Well, this statement says that you no longer get to do that. Everybody in the organization participates in the program.

DATA GOVERNANCE PLANNING SUMMARY

Objectives are the cornerstone of your program. You will use them to define your program, align to your organization's initiatives, define roles and responsibilities, identify participants, measure program outcomes, and communicate program metrics and achievements. I will say it one last time, objectives are the most important input to your program. If you cannot align something you are doing to a defined objective, it is noise for your program. You need to stop the activity or re-think the objectives. Program objectives need to be addressed on a defined cadence as needs and challenges evolve over time. If you are part of an operational program and do not have defined objectives, gather the team and write them down.

Guiding principles are also important in setting direction and guardrails for the program. They serve as a great reminder about what behaviors are okay and what are not, as well as how the program will operate. Reflective of your organization's values, they will serve as that cornerstone of values for your program.

How long does it take to define objectives and guiding principles? My guess is you can use the examples I have provided and set aside a few afternoons to put pen to paper and then cycle through for the right level of buy-in.

CHAPTER **7**

Organizational
Framework

RESULTS YOU CAN EXPECT WHEN THERE IS NO DEFINED ORGANIZATIONAL STRUCTURE

Without a defined organizational structure, people do not know what they are supposed to do or where they fit in. Because they do not know what is expected of them, they either do what they think is best or — worst case — they do nothing. The larger the intended reach of Data Governance is, the riskier it is to not think about the organizational structure.

ORGANIZATIONAL FRAMEWORK ROLES

I coach customers to not get too hung up on the exact titles of participating bodies. The title needs to resonate with the organization, which means there is an organizational culture aspect to what the bodies need to be called. A lot of organizations will start with forming a Council and then appointing Data Stewards. This is done with little thought as to how the roles are going to operate, collaborate, make decisions, communicate, or provide support. A better approach to building your organizational structure is to start with the four necessary functions of a Data Governance ecosystem. Consider the following (Figure 7.1).

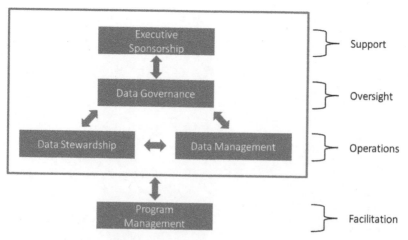

Figure 7.1 The Data Governance Ecosystem.

Support

The Data Governance program needs to be **supported** at the highest level of the organization. This **support** comes by way of providing funding, enabling resources to participate, and resolving conflicts if they arise. This is typically a role for senior leadership. Luckily, in most organizations, this **support** function already exists. Many times, we ask senior leaders to expand the focus of their **support to data-related activities**.

I am often asked where Data Governance should "live." My answer is that the program needs the **support** at a level with funding authority. So the answer depends on the reach of the program. At the enterprise level, that means someone in or very close to the C-suite. At the department or line of business level, that means the department or division leader.

Oversight

Oversight comes in many forms with many different names. I have seen it called the Data Governance Council, Data Governance Sub-Committee, Data Owner Team, Data Oversight Committee, Data Manager Team, and Data Governance Oversight Team. More important than the name is the level within the organization of the individuals. This is a decision-making body that has to have the right level of organizational authority to be accountable to program outcomes. Hence, the **oversight**. This includes resource assignment, project authority, and some level of budget authority. Why are there so many name options? Because the name of the group needs to resonate with your organization.

Operations

The two main **operational** groups in any program are Data Stewardship and Data Management. These are the people tasked with day-to-day **operations** of the program. Data Stewardship **operations** tend to be in the development and monitoring of data policies, defining data and business rules, and acting as a conduit between business and IT stakeholders. Data Management **operations** have a focus on implementing solutions that support compliance with the Data Governance policies. This includes data discovery, data quality, metadata, and database development and maintenance.

Facilitation

Lastly, the role of **facilitation** needs to be addressed. The broader the scope of Data Governance, the more important this role becomes. **Facilitation** ensures consistent communication and alignment within and across the different stakeholder groups. In some organizations, this is a dedicated role. In others, it might be an assigned project manager from a Project Management Office. If an organization adds headcount to support Data Governance, this is typically an addition.

I am not suggesting that you need to build out five groups or committees. It means that the people who are slotted into roles understand what they need to do for the program and where they fit into the Data Governance ecosystem. I have worked with organizations where the people in the **support** role also provided **oversight**. Another where an individual from **operations** provided program **facilitation**. What will work best for your circumstances? It is going to depend on the size of your organization and the expected reach of your Data Governance program. The takeaway here is that each of the roles needs to be filled, even if by the same people.

DEFINING A FRAMEWORK

Each set of roles in the Data Governance organization has clearly delineated responsibilities. This role demarcation is essential to the smooth operation of the Data Governance program since it sets the expectations for how each role functions relative to the others. By laying out these expectations, participants get clarification on what they are responsible for and what activities they can rely on others to perform. Role definition ensures that there is no ambiguity in how the Data Governance organization drives toward rapid resolution of data issues.

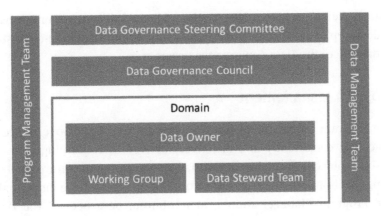

Figure 7.2 Sample Data Governance Organizational Framework.

The sample organizational framework shown in Figure 7.2 is a good starting point. This model is shown as data domain specific (e.g., customer, product, vendor, etc.) but can also be utilized at a department, line of business, or even enterprise level. The idea is that there is accountability at the domain level with representation at the enterprise level for shared data. Defined Data Owners manage within their domain and have the authority to establish working teams and appoint Data Stewards. Program Management and Data Management are shared functions to ensure consistent processes across domains from an operational and outcome perspective.

While thinking about the organizational structure, you also need to be able to describe what it means to be part of one of these bodies. I am not talking about detailed roles and responsibilities (that comes later), but you need to define enough that participants have a general understanding of what they will be asked to do.

The following section describes the sample organizational framework. This framework will be used in future chapters for detailed role definition.

Data Governance Steering Committee

The purpose of the Data Governance Steering Committee is to provide strategic guidance and foster a cooperative environment to support

Data Governance execution. Their guidance will ensure enterprise-wide acceptance of Data Governance and support the long-term sustainability of the Data Governance program.

Program Management

The Program Management function ensures that Data Governance is executing consistently and effectively as well as continuing to meet business objectives and key performance indicators across the organization. This is a permanent group comprised of one or more individuals. The Program Manager should, at minimum, be a peer of the Data Owners and has the authority to enforce Data Governance operating procedures and arbitrate issue resolution.

Data Owner

The Data Owner is an individual or group of key stakeholders that represent data in support of a given focus area (in this example, a data domain like customer or product). They will have the authority to make decisions about the data and create working teams of individuals from business and IT to effectively resolve issues. The Data Owner will also direct the work of Data Stewards.

Why the distinction of an individual or group? Because some data domains can be very large. One such example comes from a bank I worked with. The Customer domain was broken down into "core attribututes," "demographics," and "CRM." The three representatives made up the Data Owner Team for Customer, and one of them was also tasked with representing the whole domain at the enterprise level.

Working Group

Working Groups are composed of individuals from both business and IT for the purpose of solving business needs at the domain level. They can also be formed to research and make recommendations on data issues as they arise. Working Groups might also support data requirements for various projects that impact their domain. Data Stewards may or may not be part of a Working Group. The Data Owner appoints these teams.

Data Stewardship

Data Stewards leverage their business and technical domain knowledge of business processes, integration points, and data quality issues to develop business rules and definitions, identify compliance issues, and make rule recommendations. There can be one or more Data Stewards per domain or focus area. They have a clearly defined scope of authority and are identified as the go-to person for data issues and data knowledge. Data Stewards will take direction from the Data Owner within their domain or area of focus. The successful Data Steward must be an effective leader and advocate for the data management organization.

Data Management

The Data Management team focuses on the technical aspects of managing data assets. Data Management is responsible for maintaining the integrity of the data, managing the physical databases, and managing the data management tool set. Data Management implements data policies, standards, and procedures to properly manage enterprise data.

ALIGNING THE MODEL TO EXISTING STRUCTURES

Not all programs start from scratch. In fact, most organizations I work with have something that can be leveraged as a starting point for Data Governance activities. Consider the model below (Figure 7.3). It is from a college I worked with, and in the end, they just needed a kick-start to formalize roles and decided to utilize the domain model I showed before as a starting point for their organization. Note that the names look different, but the descriptions are similar to the domain model. This is because there was no reason to confuse the organization by adding new roles to do the same job. They also included an additional step of defining each data domain.

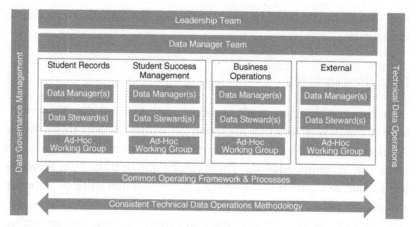

Figure 7.3 Sample Data Governance Organizational Framework.

Leadership Team

The purpose of the Leadership Team is to provide strategic guidance and create a cooperative environment to support Data Governance execution. Their guidance will ensure institution-wide acceptance of Data Governance and support its long-term sustainability.

This is a permanent group comprised of senior leadership.

Data Manager Team

The Data Manager Team is accountable for oversight of data assets and processes.

This is a permanent group comprised of Data Managers to ensure that cross-domain visibility and decision making is in place for institution-wide data.

Domain Definitions — Student

The Student data domain is subdivided into Student Records (SR) and Student Success Management (SSM). SR encompasses factual dimensions like enrollment, financial aid, accounts receivable, and non-credit coursework. SSM is more peripheral to these core components and reflects services such as appointments, polls or surveys, notes, and academic planning.

Domain Definitions — Business Operations

Business Operations data domain reflects institutional assets such as facilities, equipment, courses, programs, faculty, staff, human resources, and information technology. In other words, this domain encompasses functional units that allow the college to offer its core programs and services.

Domain Definitions — External

The External data domain reflects outward-facing activities such as marketing and interactions with alumni, donors, corporations, advisory boards, and vendors. In other words, this domain encompasses relationship management.

Data Manager

The Data Manager is accountable for oversight of data assets and processes within their domain. They align business and IT efforts for any technical data operations. The Data Manager is an individual or small group with the authority to make decisions about domain data and appoint Data Stewards and Ad-Hoc Working Groups to effectively research and resolve issues as well as monitor and recommend policies.

The Data Manager will represent their domain on the Data Manager Team to ensure cross-domain communication and collaboration on data efforts.

Data Steward

Data Stewards leverage their business and technical domain knowledge of business processes, integration points, and data quality issues to develop business rules and definitions, identify compliance issues, and make policy recommendations. They will be recognized as the go-to person for data issues and data knowledge within a domain.

Data Stewards will take direction from the Data Manager and guidance from Data Governance Management. There can be more than one Data Steward per domain. In some cases, a Data Steward may also be a Data Manager.

Ad-Hoc Working Group

Ad-Hoc Working Groups are composed of business and IT individuals for the purpose of solving business needs at the domain level. They can be formed as needed to research and make recommendations on data issues.

These temporary groups are appointed by the Data Manager(s) for a domain. They may be comprised of subject matter experts, key stakeholders, and/or technical resources.

Data Governance Management

Data Governance Management ensures that Data Governance is executing consistently and effectively. This function will also communicate performance indicators and program metrics across domains.

This is a permanent group comprised of one or more individuals.

Technical Data Operations

Technical Data Operations focuses on the technical aspects of managing data assets such as maintaining the integrity of the data, managing physical databases, and curating the data management tool set.

This function will implement data policies, standards, and procedures to properly manage data across domains.

ALIGNING THE FRAMEWORK TO THE CULTURE

The organizational framework has to resonate with its intended audience, no matter where they are in the organization. I was helping a customer in the Dominican Republic with their Data Governance program. The organization was embarking on a new reporting and analytic platform that was not allowed to be called a Data Warehouse because a previous data warehousing project had failed. They wanted to ensure any data that landed on the new platform was subject to Data Governance oversight.

Everybody in that organization wore a suit, every day. In addition to noticing the suits, I noticed several people had lapel pins. I thought they were some type of country pride pin or had something to do with baseball (the Caribbean World Series was in full swing at the time). It was neither of those. If you had a gold pin, you were an executive. If you had a silver pin, you were a senior leader. If you had a blue pin, you had managerial responsibilities. Nothing happened in that organization without the backing of a gold pin. Here is what their organizational framework looked like (Figure 7.4).

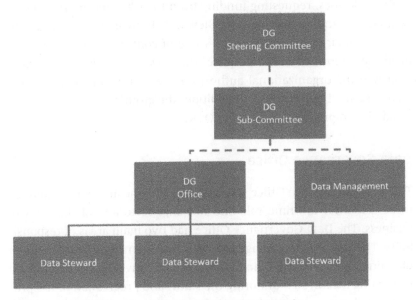

Figure 7.4 Sample Data Governance Organizational Framework.

It looks a lot like an organizational structure. In that particular organization with their culture, it needed to. There were some role definition commonalities and differences with this Data Governance organization structure. Some may resonate with your organization, some may not.

Data Governance Steering Committee

Instead of creating an entire new body for providing oversight, we extended the charter of an existing Operations and Technology Committee (OTR) made up of executive leadership in the bank. This was the team of "gold pins." Utilizing existing decision-making bodies can be a great starting point as long as the participants have the correct level of organizational authority.

Data Governance Sub-Committee

This group was comprised of key business stakeholders who were division managers with an analytical focus. The group was tasked with setting priorities, requesting funding from the OTR, monitoring policy compliance, and identifying Data Stewards. Individuals were asked to represent their line of business or scope of control and balance those needs and priorities with enterprise strategies and needs. Each participant had the organizational authority to carry this out because they were a team of "silver pins." In addition, the group was chaired by one "gold pin" to provide a link to the OTR.

Data Governance Office

The Data Governance Office was comprised of one individual intended to be a neutral full-time role and not aligned to any of the lines of business. The Data Governance Office had two main areas of responsibility. The first was to manage the Data Governance program through planning and executing Data Governance initiatives, coordinating and facilitating meetings, monitoring the status and progression of the program, and communicating standards and guidelines. The second was supervising the Data Stewardship Team.

This is the only organization I have worked with that had full-time dedicated Data Stewards combined into one team with a direct reporting relationship to the Data Governance program management function. A reason for this was the program management office understood data priorities and could direct the work of the Data Stewards (right color pin). It also ensured that the Data Stewards' tasks would not be overruled by other managers in the business areas.

Data Steward

The Data Steward role was a standard set of data stewardship activities. The initial focus was on defining terms, gathering metadata, and establishing data quality practices using a pre-defined tool set. The Data Stewards were moved into the organizational structure because of their expertise with certain data domains or processes. There were also folks who had the ability to collaborate across different lines of business in the bank, which is an important characteristic of any Data Steward. Because of the hierarchical nature of the organization, the Data Governance Office (manager of the team) was tasked with activities where a Data Steward might not have the right level of authority. In other words, the Data Steward defined data acceptance criteria, but the Data Governance Office was on the hook for establishing data remediation service level agreements with leaders in various lines of business.

SIMPLIFYING THE MODEL

Does it feel too arduous to draw a picture and write paragraphs describing each decision-making body? Here is another example that outlines what each role does right on the framework itself. Again, the goal here is that the different groups know what is going to be asked of them (Figure 7.5).

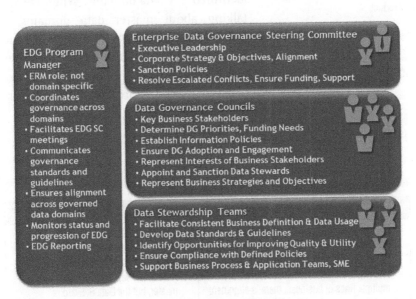

Figure 7.5 Sample Data Governance Organizational Framework.

DEFINING THE RIGHT DATA STEWARDSHIP MODEL

Like everything else, defining the right framework for your organization depends on what you want to achieve. Yes, right back to program objectives. And you need to consider where the role of the Data Steward fits in. That is because the work of the Data Steward is central to the day-to-day operations of your program.

The following sections are examples of data stewardship models. Each model has pros and cons. I offer these pros and cons as a way for you to think about your own organization and how you might want to build your program to best leverage the Data Stewardship role and how it will work within your existing organizational structure and culture.

Data Domain Model

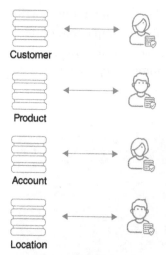

The data domain model aligns Data Stewards to defined data subject areas such as customer, product, or account. This model is ideal for master data management programs or organizations with identified key data domains. When we are talking about master data domains, I always recommend beginning with the minimum set of attributions; in other words, the fewest number of attributes necessary to be shared across the enterprise (Table 7.1).

Table 7.1 Data Domain Model Pros and Cons.

Pros	Cons
▪ The model is business driven because the master domains are core to the organization's business processes. ▪ Because the master domains support multiple lines of business, there is alignment at the enterprise level. In other words, the entirety of the organization cares about customer data.	▪ Appointed Data Stewards may not necessarily report to the same management group. For example, Marketing may "own" the customer master, but the Data Steward is from Finance.

Table 7.1 (*Continued*)

Pros	Cons
■ With a single definition of key data domains, there is inherent consistency across different processes, functions, and systems. If not at first, it is a clear goal of the Data Governance program. ■ The data boundaries are clear. Data attributes can be aligned to an adopted definition, so the scope of Data Governance is absolute – the data that supports the definition. ■ The size of Data Steward teams may be smaller with this model, especially for smaller data domains. ■ The model is flexible because of the confined scope. As definitions change over time (e.g., augmenting customer master data with additional attributes), the changes are occurring in one location as opposed to many systems across the enterprise.	■ This model requires consistent data management execution across domains. Typically, IT functions are a shared service, and that means there should be common processes regarding interactions between Data Stewards and developers, regardless of the domain. ■ Some domains may be large and complex. Taking on too much at the onset of your program can lead to immediate failures. Again, choose the smallest amount of data to oversee and expand from there. ■ If Data Stewards are focused on nothing but the master data, they may lose focus on wider enterprise initiatives that may impact their domain. Communication across domains and enterprise initiatives can alleviate this risk.

Business Function Model

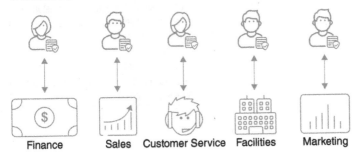

The business function, or organization model, aligns Data Stewards to departments, divisions, or lines of business depending on the size of the organization. Examples may include Finance, Marketing, Sales, Customer Service, or Facilities. While not at the enterprise level, this model is ideal for expediting Data Governance within a given department. That way, more mature departments can begin efforts and the program can expand to other departments over time. I recommend this as a starting point, not an end point, for any program because more often than not, data is required across departments in order to provide value (Table 7.2).

Table 7.2 Business Function Model Pros and Cons.

Pros	Cons
▪ These are business-focused departments so there is a natural business orientation. ▪ Because the Data Stewards are focused on a department they already work in, there is no conflict with existing organizational structures. If there are, they can be handled within the confines of the department itself. ▪ Functional control of Data Governance activities is maintained within the given department. The program is not reliant on other departments for activities and decision making. ▪ Data Stewards already have context and expertise because they have "the history" in the department. ▪ Consensus can be easier because program activities stay within department leadership's sphere of control.	▪ There can be a lack of enterprise perspective when activities are limited to the confines of a given department. ▪ When too many departments begin their own efforts, there may be conflicting policies and more importantly, definitions of key data. Communication and agreement across departments becomes crucial. ▪ Finance needs access to Sales data for planning and projections. Marketing needs access to Sales data to better design campaigns. Customer Service needs to understand the history of the customer when they call. Facilities needs to understand what they need to plan to build. The point here is that different business areas need to share data from the same applications. Again, communication and agreement across departments become crucial. ▪ Accountabilities for data domains may cross departmental boundaries. Customer data is most likely used, updated, or augmented by multiple departments. Planning who can do what to which data is very important so departments do not begin to create their own data silos of what should be shared data.

Application Model

The application model aligns Data Stewards to applications and is a good starting point for an organization with large complex applications. Examples might be Customer Relationship Management (CRM), Enterprise Resource Planning (ERP), Financials, or even an Enterprise

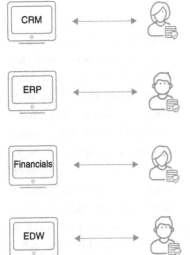

Data Warehouse (EDW) or some other reporting and analytic platform. Some of these applications can be daunting because of their size and complexity. Think of the modules in an ERP system. My experience has mostly seen focus on EDWs because that is the place where data is integrated and therefore where most issues are identified. If starting with an EDW as a focus, take the time to define which data subject areas fall under Data Governance (Table 7.3).

Table 7.3 Application Model Pros and Cons.

Pros	Cons
• There is clearly defined ownership for an application, both from the business perspective and perhaps a product owner from the IT side. • Data Stewards work in the applications so they are familiar with the workflows of data in the system. • With the exception of reporting and analytic platforms, this model focuses on data at the "system or origin." • The scope of an application provides immediate scope for a Data Governance program, making program participants easier to onboard than some of the other models.	• The focus on a single application immediately limits the reach of Data Governance beyond the confines of the application itself. Communication and representative decision making across all users will need to be considered. • This model can limit the broader business usage of the data because the focus is on the application data itself. The application's goal may or may not be aware of data implications to downstream systems or even to business measurement. • Without constant communication, this model can promote silos in both processes and data outputs that usually stem from differing definitions.

Project Model

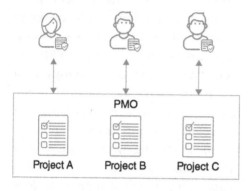

Before anything else, it is important to point out that Data Governance is a program and not a project. However, the project model can work well for a quick launch in support of high-impact projects. Projects tend to come with funding and resources and Data Governance processes can help solve for data-related issues that seem to get in the way of many projects we've all worked on. Like the other models, this is a starting point for Data Governance (Table 7.4).

Table 7.4 Project Model Pros and Cons.

Pros	Cons
▪ Projects have sponsors so there is clearly defined ownership. Most organizations have formal project management methodologies that include communication so it can be a good mechanism for communicating about Data Governance activities to gain buy-in for ongoing support. ▪ Projects have funding and resources so there is not a perceived intrusion on staff that may have many things on their to-do list. The time dedicated to the Data Governance effort is time they can bill against the project.	▪ Projects end. And when they end, the resources are reassigned. For Data Governance to be sustainable, there has to be a plan in place to transcend project boundaries. ▪ Multiple projects attempting Data Governance as part of their project may not be aware of each other's efforts. That can result in duplicative or even conflicting processes or results. ▪ Data Governance adoption is at risk because of the confines of project work. Again, resources are reassigned at project close, and the responsibilities that Data Governance may have established now belong to no one.

ORGANIZATIONAL FRAMEWORK SUMMARY

Defining an organizational framework is important. Program participants will better understand how they fit into the program structure and what they will be asked to do. Because that initial understanding is there, the participants are more likely to do just that — participate. The goal of the organizational framework is to visually describe the different decision-making bodies and how they are expected to interact with each other. The framework needs to have sufficient detail or be simplified enough so that it is easily consumable by all stakeholders, whether or not they are active program participants. This initial role definition is not meant to replace detailed program responsibilities. That is the next step.

CHAPTER 8

Roles and
Responsibilities

RESULTS YOU CAN EXPECT WHEN ROLES AND RESPONSIBILITIES ARE NOT CLEARLY DEFINED

In Chapter 7, "Organizational Framework," I wrote about the importance of designing the organizational framework and providing definition around each of the decision-making bodies in the framework. That activity is not meant to take the place of defining detailed roles and responsibilities. If you skip this step, the participants will not have clear direction on the tasks they need to do, decisions they need to make, or oversight they need to provide. The end-result of not knowing is chaos, which means that skipping this step dooms your program.

ALIGNING ACTIONS AND DECISIONS TO PROGRAM OBJECTIVES

Defining key activities and decisions is the first step to detailed roles and responsibilities. This step is best taken without considering who is going to do the work. How do you determine the types of activities or decisions? Start with your objectives. I like to organize objectives by Data Management capabilities (Data Architecture, Metadata, Data Quality, Data Administration, Reporting & Analytics, Reference & Master Data, Data Security, and Data Life Cycle) and Data Governance program functions (Strategy & Alignment, Establish Data Governance Program, and Data Governance Operations). Table 8.1 shows the sample objectives we defined earlier grouped by the Data Management capabilities and Data Governance functions I just outlined. You do not have to take this step; I do it because it helps me stay organized.

Table 8.1 Data Management Functions Aligned to Program Objectives.

Data Management Function	Objective
▪ Establish Data Governance Program ▪ Data Governance Operations ▪ Strategy & Alignment	Establish an organizational framework with clear roles and responsibilities that enable sustainable execution across multiple domains
▪ Data Architecture	Ensure core data domains are integrated into single versions to support reporting/analytic needs across departments

Table 8.1 (Continued)

Data Management Function	Objective
▪ Data Quality	Increase the overall trust in data through implementation of a data quality process
▪ Metadata	Establish a metadata process to ensure business rules, policies, documents, and news are accessible and searchable across departments
▪ Communication	Generate awareness around the use of the data, its value, and the need for governance
▪ Data Quality	Assign clear authority and accountability for data assets
▪ Metadata	Maintain a consistent definition of the data and its business rules
▪ Reference & Master Data	Eliminate redundant or conflicting business processes and practices

That was the easy part. The next step is to define the activities and decisions. This is still not the time to try and define who is going to be doing the activity. It is time to think about the activities that will help achieve the objective. I have added the activities that align to each of the objectives in the tables that follow. The lists are meant to be examples that you can use as starting points.

Strategy & Alignment

Strategy & Alignment are essential for an effective Data Governance program. To be successful, program activities must align to overall business strategy. A sustainable program also requires support from leadership (Table 8.2).

Table 8.2 Strategy & Alignment Activities/Decisions.

Data Management Function	Activities/Decisions
Strategy & Alignment	Set strategic direction and goals for Data Governance
	Review performance of objectives, goals, status, and benefits of the program
	Coordinate and facilitate Data Governance program
	Provide program funding
	Provide overall Data Governance program sponsorship
	Set Data Governance priorities

The objective(s) of this function are:

- Establish an organizational framework with clear roles and responsibilities that enable sustainable execution across multiple domains

Establish Data Governance Program

The goal of this function is to get the Data Governance program off the ground through development of program collateral (you can see samples in this chapter and others), identify key participants, and then onboard them. I have worked with a number of customers where individuals that played a key role in designing the program were not identified as participants in the program. That is why we are starting with activities and not people. I choose to break apart "Establish Data Governance Program" and "Data Governance Operations" because once the program is established, the verbs on the tasks change. Again, it is my preference. No matter how you choose to organize, as long as you are aligned to objectives you will be in good shape (Table 8.3).

Table 8.3 Establish Data Governance Program Activities/Decisions.

Data Management Function	Activities/Decisions
Establish Data Governance Program	Identify/engage Data Governance Steering Committee members
	Identify Data Owners/Data Governance Council members
	Develop and publish Data Governance Charter
	Develop and publish workflows
	Develop and publish operating procedures
	Develop and publish communications plan
	Develop Data Governance training
	Deliver Data Governance training material
	Onboard program participants
	Develop intake and prioritization process

The objective(s) of this function are:

- Establish an organizational framework with clear roles and responsibilities that enable sustainable execution across multiple domains
- Generate awareness around the use of the data, its value, and the need for governance

Data Governance Operations

This function represents the ongoing program management tasks such as onboarding, communicating, and updating key program collateral. Some of the activities are similar to "Establish Data Governance Program" but you will notice the verbs have changed (Table 8.4).

Table 8.4 Data Governance Operations Activities/Decisions.

Data Management Function	Activities/Decisions
Data Governance Operations	Identify/engage Data Governance Steering Committee members
	Identify Data Owners/Data Governance Council members
	Review, identify, and "onboard" Data Stewards
	Update Data Governance Charter
	Update workflows
	Develop and publish operating procedures
	Update training materials
	Update communications plan
	Deliver Data Governance training
	Onboard program participants
	Launch Data Governance program communications
	Develop Data Governance program metrics
	Publish Data Governance program metrics
	Monitor compliance with policies
	Communicate policy compliance and progress
	Arbitrate disputes across stakeholder groups
	Maintain consolidated issue list
	Facilitate communication across domains

The objective(s) of this function are:

- Establish an organizational framework with clear roles and responsibilities that enables sustainable execution across multiple domains
- Generate awareness around the use of the data, its value, and the need for governance

Data Architecture

Policies for data architecture should align to a defined data strategy that includes a plan for identifying, provisioning, storing, and integrating data. The activities in this part of the list should enable or reinforce what is in that data strategy (Table 8.5).

Table 8.5 Data Architecture Activities/Decisions.

Data Management Function	Activities/Decisions
Data Architecture	Establish and maintain data models
	Define data strategy
	Develop and document standards for data movement
	Establish data architecture as a formalized process to enhance data integration
	Adopt a single ETL tool that supports standardized ETL
	Align policies to software development life cycle
	Develop data standards
	Enforce data standards

The objective of this function is:

- Ensure core data domains are integrated into single versions to support reporting/analytic needs across departments

Metadata

There are several tasks with the gathering, updating, and publishing of metadata. I do not recommend adding all those verbs into one line because different roles will more than likely take on different activities. Taking the time to think about how the metadata process aligns to the organizational framework will help the process of defining roles and responsibilities in the policy itself later on (Table 8.6).

Table 8.6 Metadata Activities/Decisions.

Data Management Function	Activities/Decisions
Metadata	Develop metadata policy
	Approve metadata policy
	Monitor compliance to metadata policy
	Collect technical metadata
	Create business metadata
	Publish metadata
	Maintain metadata
	Maintain a searchable repository that is easily accessible by business stakeholders

The objective of this function is:

■ Establish a metadata process to ensure business rules, policies, documents, and news are accessible and searchable across departments

Data Quality

The goal of any data quality process is to increase the reliability and usability of data. Like the other activities, I recommend breaking down the lines by the verbs because the group creating a policy might not necessarily be the group who approves it (Table 8.7).

Table 8.7 Data Quality Program Activities/Decisions.

Data Management Function	Activities/Decisions
Data Quality	Create data quality policy
	Approve data quality policy
	Publish data quality policy
	Monitor compliance to data quality policy
	Define data quality business rules

(Continued)

Table 8.7 (Continued)

Data Management Function	Activities/Decisions
Data Quality (Continued)	Implement data quality business rules
	Establish data quality baseline
	Define data quality metrics
	Report and publish data quality status
	Remediate data quality issues
	Identify and prioritize key data to be monitored
	Identify and recommend technology solutions to support data quality process
	Perform data profiling
	Identify data quality issues, root causes, and proposed remediation
	Establish data quality service level agreements

The objective(s) of this function are:

- Increase the overall trust in data through implementation of a data quality process
- Assign clear authority and accountability for data assets

Reference & Master Data

Master Data Management is a set of processes, technologies, and policies used to create, maintain, and manage data associated with core business entities. If you are going down a master data path, I recommend you also take a good look at the data architecture, metadata, and data quality activities as well (Table 8.8).

Table 8.8 Reference & Master Data Activities/Decisions.

Data Management Function	Activities
Reference & Master Data	Develop master data policy
	Approve master data policy
	Monitor compliance with master data policies
	Define master domains
	Define reference data
	Define quality and validation
	Define and modify business rules for establishing master record (e.g., matching, merging, survivorship)

Table 8.8 (*Continued*)

Data Management Function	Activities
Reference & Master Data (*Continued*)	Define data provisioning standards
	Monitor and report master data metrics (data quality, performance, etc.)

The objective of this function is:

- Eliminate redundant or conflicting business processes and practices

USING A RACI MODEL

We have finished identifying activities and decisions that will help us achieve our program objectives. The next step is the hardest part in designing a Data Governance program. That is because we are identifying activities that someone will ultimately be held accountable for. We are also looking at potentially changing people's day-to-day activities.

To help with this process, I like to use the RACI model. The RACI (Responsible, Accountable, Consulted, or Informed) matrixes identify specific sets of activities and their respective responsibilities. Only one role is Accountable for the activity, whereas several other roles may be involved in carrying out the work or being consulted or informed during the course of the work. This approach serves to prevent everyone being involved (solving the "too many cooks" problem) and assigns accountability to one and only one individual or group.

Here is a description of each of the letters in the model:

R	Responsible	Does the work
A	Accountable	Ensures the work is done/approver
C	Consulted	Provides input
I	Informed	Notified, not active participant

One challenge my customers have in this exercise is jumping to people. We are still not at a point where we are naming names. That comes later. We need to consider the activity and identify one column for Accountability. I will demonstrate in the follow-on sections how to use the RACI model for identifying people and developing Data Governance workflows.

As a reminder, the columns in the tables are aligned to the organizational framework we defined. Here is a legend:

PM	Program Management
DGSC	Data Governance Steering Committee
DGC	Data Governance Council
DO	Data Owner
WG	Working Group
DS	Data Steward
DM	Data Management Team

Strategy & Alignment

The DGSC is accountable for overall program oversight, funding, and direction while the DGC sets Data Governance priorities that then align to that direction. The PM function ensures coordination across domains and ongoing review of program status (Table 8.9).

Table 8.9 Strategy & Alignment RACI.

Data Management Function	Activities	PM	DGSC	DGC	DO	WG	DS	DM
Strategy & Alignment	Set strategic direction and goals for Data Governance	C	A	R	R	C	I	I
	Review performance of objectives, goals, status, and benefits of the program	A	I	C	R	R	C	I
	Coordinate and facilitate Data Governance program	A	I	C	R	R	C	I
	Provide program funding	C	A	R	C	C	I	C
	Provide overall Data Governance program sponsorship	C	A	R	R	I	I	I
	Set Data Governance priorities	C	C	A	R	I	C	C

Establish Data Governance Program

Most accountability is at the DGC level for establishing the program. The DOs are listed as consulted because they make up the DGC. There will be a lot of to-do's for the PM function as this is a time where key program collateral is developed (Table 8.10).

Table 8.10 Establish Data Governance Program RACI.

Data Management Function	Activities	PM	DGSC	DGC	DO	WG	DS	DM
Establish Data Governance Program	Identify/engage Data Governance Steering Committee members	R	A	I	I	I	I	I
	Identify Data Owners/ Data Governance Council members	R	A	I	I	I	I	I
	Develop and publish Data Governance Charter	R	C	A	C	I	I	I
	Develop and publish workflows	R	C	A	C	I	I	I
	Develop and publish operating procedures	R	I	A	C	I	C	C
	Develop and publish communications plan	R	I	A	C	I	I	I
	Develop Data Governance training	R	I	A	C	I	I	I
	Deliver Data Governance training material	A	I	R	R	I	R	R
	Onboard program participants	C	I	A	R	I	R	R
	Develop intake and prioritization process	R	I	A	R	I	C	C

Data Governance Program Operations

As the Data Governance program becomes operational, it is up to the DGC to provide updates for how the program needs to function and where to focus activities. They will achieve this by working collectively as DOs and consulting with the PM, DS, and DM teams (Table 8.11).

Table 8.11 Data Governance Operations RACI.

Data Management Function	Activities	PM	DGSC	DGC	DO	WG	DS	DM
Data Governance Program Operations	Identify/engage Data Governance Steering Committee members	R	A	I	I	I	I	I
	Identify Data Owners/Data Governance Council members	R	A	I	I	I	I	I
	Review, identify, and "onboard" Data Stewards	C	I	I	A	C	C	C
	Update Data Governance Charter	R	I	A	R	I	C	I
	Update workflows	R	I	A	R	I	C	I
	Update operating procedures	R	I	A	R	I	C	C
	Update training materials	R	I	A	I	I	C	C
	Update communications plan	A	I	R	R	I	C	C
	Deliver Data Governance training	C	I	A	R	I	R	R
	Onboard program participants	A	I	R	R	I	R	R
	Launch Data Governance program communications	A	I	R	R	I	R	R
	Develop Data Governance program metrics	R	C	R	C	I	R	R
	Publish Data Governance program metrics	R	I	A	R	I	R	R
	Communicate policy compliance and progress	R	I	A	C	I	R	R
	Monitor compliance with policies	C	I	A	R	R	R	I
	Grant policy compliance waiver	I	I	A	R	C	C	R
	Arbitrate disputes across stakeholder groups	I	A	R	C	I	I	C
	Maintain consolidated issue list	A	I	I	R	R	R	R
	Facilitate communication across domains	A	I	R	R	R	C	R

Data Architecture

Although the DGC is accountable to ensure these activities are happening, the DM team has the responsibility for developing the models, defining standards, and adopting Data Management tools (Table 8.12).

Table 8.12 Data Architecture RACI.

Data Management Function	Activities	PM	DGSC	DGC	DO	WG	DS	DM
Data Architecture	Establish and maintain data models	I	I	A	C	I	R	R
	Define data strategy	I	I	A	C	I	C	R
	Develop and document standards for data movement	I	I	A	C	I	C	R
	Establish data architecture as a formalized process to enhance data integration	I	I	A	C	I	C	R
	Adopt a single ETL tool that supports standardized ETL	I	I	A	C	I	C	R
	Align policies to software development life cycle	R	I	A	R	C	C	C
	Develop data standards	I	I	A	C	C	C	R
	Enforce data standards	I	I	A	C	C	C	R

Metadata

The DOs, along with support from the DS and DM teams are responsible for metadata within their domain. They may even establish WGs to consult for creating metadata if there are dataset beyond the knowledge of the identified DS (Table 8.13).

Table 8.13 Metadata RACI.

Data Management Function	Activities	PM	DGSC	DGC	DO	WG	DS	DM
Metadata	Develop metadata policy	I	I	C	A	C	R	R
	Approve metadata policy	C	I	A	R	I	I	I
	Monitor compliance to metadata policy	A	I	I	R	I	R	R
	Collect technical metadata	C	I	A	C	C	C	R
	Create business metadata	C	I	A	R	C	R	C
	Publish metadata	A	I	C	C	I	C	R
	Maintain metadata	C	I	A	R	C	R	C
	Maintain a searchable repository that is easily accessible by business stakeholders	I	I	A	R	I	R	R

Data Quality

Data quality responsibilities lie with the DS team in a given domain and the shared DM function. The DO may be consulted but has oversight over compliance in their domains. WGs may be established to research broader data quality questions or issues (Table 8.14).

Reference & Master Data

Although DOs are accountable to ensure master record definition, they will often establish a WG that is made up of DS and DM team members along with business subject matter experts. DS and DM will be responsible for ongoing maintenance of the master records (Table 8.15).

Table 8.14 Data Quality RACI.

Data Management Function	Activities	PM	DGSC	DGC	DO	WG	DS	DM
Data Quality	Create data quality policy	C	I	A	R	R	R	R
	Approve data quality policy	C	I	A	R	R	I	I
	Publish data quality policy	R	I	A	I	I	I	I
	Monitor compliance to data quality policy	A	I	C	R	I	R	R
	Define data quality business rules	C	I	A	C	R	R	R
	Implement data quality business rules	I	I	A	I	I	C	R
	Establish data quality baseline	C	I	A	C	I	R	R
	Define data quality metrics	I	I	A	C	R	R	R
	Report and publish data quality status	A	I	C	R	I	R	R
	Remediate data quality issues	I	I	A	C	R	R	R
	Identify and prioritize key data to be monitored	I	I	A	R	I	R	C
	Identify and recommend technology solutions to support data quality process	I	I	A	C	I	C	R
	Perform data profiling	C	I	A	R	I	R	R
	Identify data quality issues, root causes, and proposed remediation	I	I	A	R	R	R	C
	Establish data quality service level agreements	I	I	A	R	I	C	C

Table 8.15 Reference & Master Data RACI.

Data Management Function	Activities	PM	DGSC	DGC	DO	WG	DS	DM
Reference & Master Data	Develop master data policy	C	I	A	R	R	R	C
	Approve master data policy	R	I	A	R	I	I	I
	Monitor compliance with master data policies	A	I	I	R	I	R	R
	Define master domains	C	I	C	A	R	R	R
	Define reference data	C	I	C	A	R	R	R
	Define quality and validation	C	I	A	R	I	R	C
	Define and modify business rules for establishing master record (e.g., matching, merging, survivorship)	C	I	A	R	I	C	R
	Define data provisioning standards	I	I	I	A	I	I	R
	Monitor and report master data metrics (data quality, performance, etc.)	R	I	A	R	I	R	R

DEFINING ROLES AND RESPONSIBILITIES

Now that we have completed the RACI model, we can better articulate what each group is responsible for. Continuing with our same example, we can utilize the RACI model to create more detailed roles and responsibilities for our organizational framework.

DATA GOVERNANCE STEERING COMMITTEE

Data Governance Steering Committee members are expected to:

- Provide strategy, communications, sponsorship, leadership, and active engagement to accomplish Data Governance objectives

- Create a culture of understanding the value of customer data
- Approve Data Owner Teams
- Monitor Data Governance and data quality performance metrics
- Provide executive sponsorship for Data Governance strategy and initiatives
- Maintain alignment between the organization's strategic objectives and Data Governance priorities
- Authorize the Data Owner teams to execute Data Governance decisions and activities
- Provide funding approval for Data Governance programs, resources, and solutions
- Empower Data Owner Teams to write, approve, and enforce data policies
- Act as a point of escalation, if needed, to resolve data-related issues that cannot be resolved by the Data Owner Teams
- Review Data Governance program compliance and performance measures to ensure intended objectives are met
- Foster a culture that values data as an asset by socializing and promoting the value of Data Governance and supporting/enforcing Data Governance procedures and decisions

PROGRAM MANAGEMENT

The Program Management team members are expected to:

- Facilitate and coordinate execution of Data Governance program activities
- Ensure Data Governance alignment and consistency across departments
- Support development of common operating procedures and processes (e.g., intake and prioritization, standard document templates)
- Develop and execute a comprehensive Data Governance program communication plan
- Monitor the status and progress of Data Governance including creation and publication of regular program status reports

- Support development of Data Governance program metrics and measures
- Educate stakeholders and increase awareness of Data Governance processes across City departments
- Develop, update, and deliver Data Governance training materials
- Communicate Data Owner Team updates, issues, and funding requests to the Data Governance Steering Committee
- Gather, collect, maintain, and publish Data Governance issue list
- Define, update, and modify Data Governance artifacts (charter, templates, workflows, etc.)
- Ensure publication of business and technical metadata
- Ensure publication of all Data Governance program artifacts
- Monitor and report risks regarding program
- Nominate department-level data owners

DATA GOVERNANCE COUNCIL

Members of the Data Governance Council are expected to:

- Ensure DG information policies and practices align with senior leadership vision
- Oversee DG activities
- Establish working teams (business and technical SMEs) to define DG cross-domain policies
- Provide support for cross-domain projects
- Arbitrate DG policy-related issues escalated from the domains
- Review the performance of the objectives, goals, status, and benefits of the program
- Ensure adoption of information policies and processes within the department
- Request necessary funding to enable DG initiatives
- Oversee the development and maintenance of DG operating procedures and workflows

- Grant formal waivers for policy non-compliance
- Ensure all DG program activities are completed per approved policies, procedures, and standards

DATA OWNER TEAM

Data Owner team members are expected to:

- Represent their domain/focus area on the Data Governance Council
- Ensure Data Governance information rules and practices align with senior leadership vision
- Oversee Data Governance activities
- Establish working teams (business and technical SMEs) to define Data Governance cross-domain rules
- Provide support for cross-domain projects
- Review the performance of the objectives, goals, status, and benefits of the program
- Ensure adoption of information rules and processes within the department
- Request necessary funding to enable Data Governance initiatives
- Oversee the development and maintenance of Data Governance operating procedures and workflows
- Grant formal waivers for rule non-compliance
- Ensure all Data Governance program activities are completed per approved rules, procedures, and standards
- Identify and appoint Data Steward team members
- Ensure appropriate Data Steward direction, training, and support
- Assign, manage, and prioritize work within their focus area
- Establish a data quality process that includes profiling, data quality KPIs, monitoring, SLAs, and issue remediation for their customer data within their agency
- Approve domain-specific data policies and KPIs
- Create and maintain focus-area metadata

WORKING GROUP

Working Group team members are expected to:

- Provide support to remediate data issues
- Provide expertise on domain data
- Recommend and help develop data policies, procedures, and standards
- Ensure information is collected, shared, reused, and defined in a manner that will benefit the department
- Develop and monitor Data Governance performance metrics and measures
- Review/resolve issues escalated from the Data Steward team
- Escalate any unresolved data issues to Data Owner

DATA STEWARDSHIP

Data Steward team members are expected to:

- Create and maintain domain business metadata
- Recommend data quality metrics (KPIs) for key data
- Monitor and report on domain Data Governance metrics
- Remediate data quality issues and recommend data quality controls
- Monitor and report compliance to Data Governance rules
- Create domain and department Data Governance rules
- Communicate the value of data to the user community
- Identify issues to the Data Owner
- Act as point of contact for focus area data questions
- Align data quality activities to the Data Governance data quality rules
- Define key domain attributes and metadata

DATA MANAGEMENT

Data Management team members are expected to:

- Act as the central contact point for all data management activities
- Oversee process for data change management
- Create and maintain data standards resulting from rule decisions
- Define source data extract standards for data provisioning
- Define and maintain data testing standards and development environments
- Support the Data Stewards in resolving data issues
- Provide technical data expertise to support Data Governance initiatives
- Align technology decisions with business needs
- Identify, recommend, and implement technology solutions
- Support the collection and maintenance of a searchable repository for technical metadata
- Support the monitoring and enforcement of approved data management policies
- Write data architecture policies
- Identify/create data strategy
- Evaluate, implement, and maintain DM tool set
- Define reusable data extract, transform, and load (ETL) processes

NAMING NAMES

We are still not quite ready to identify people to fill these roles (but we're close). There is one more interim step: representation. You need to decide what functional groups need to be represented in order to attach names to those roles. The other consideration is the level at which people are accountable for the activities and decisions outlined in the RACI model. Here are some examples of defining representation that will lead directly to names.

Data Governance for Product in a retail environment is to be established. The natural question is "who needs to have a seat at the table to make decisions about product?" It is not just the merchandising team.

Here is the boiled-down list:

- Customer Support Services
- Operational Controller
- Information Technology
- Marketing and Advertising
- Merchandising
- Merchandising Support
- Quality Assurance
- Supply Chain
- Store Operations Support

Considering the level of accountability for this group of product decision makers, it was deemed they needed to at least be at the vice president level. The names came easily after that.

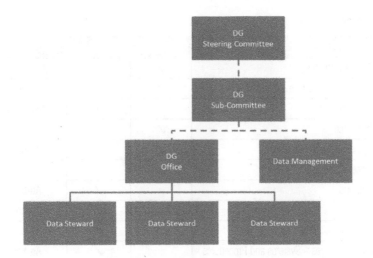

This was the organization with the pins. They focused Data Governance efforts on anything that was part of a new reporting and analytic platform. The first subject area on the platform was "Credit Card Fraud." The same question was asked. "Who needs a seat at the table to make decisions about credit card fraud?"

Their Data Governance Sub-Committee list is below, but they went a step further and decided that some members didn't need to attend every meeting or working session so they broke down who should always be represented and who might need to be represented or provide input on an as-needed basis (Table 8.16).

Table 8.16 Sample Data Governance Representation.

Stakeholder Group	Decision	Informed	Participation
Data Governance Office (coordinator)			
Credit, Market, and Liquidity Risk	✓		Permanent
Retail Business	✓		Permanent
Marketing	✓		Permanent
Operational Risk	✓		Permanent

(Continued)

Table 8.16 (Continued)

Stakeholder Group	Decision	Informed	Participation
Credit Card Business	✓		Permanent
Strategic Planning/Committee Chair	✓		Permanent
IT Development		✓	Permanent
Compliance	✓		Ad-hoc
Credit Card Fraud Prevention	✓		Ad-hoc
Finance	✓		Ad-hoc
Operations		✓	Ad-hoc
IT Architecture		✓	Ad-hoc
Information Security		✓	Ad-hoc
Human Resources – Systems and Procedures		✓	Ad-hoc

Because authority came from the pin on the lapel, the names fell into place. All participants were "silver pins" with the exception of the Strategic Planning Vice President. He was a "gold pin" and also part of their Data Governance Steering Committee.

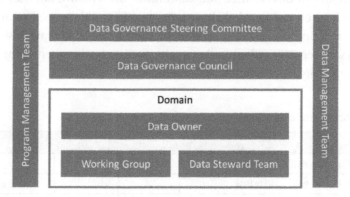

Here is the example we used for building the RACI. In this organization, the Program Management Team recommended Data Owners to the Data Governance Steering Committee. If the domains were large enough, there might be a Data Owner team within the domain that would represent the enterprise level on the Data

Governance Council. As with the other examples, the level of the Data Owner is dependent on what accountabilities they have. In our example, it is likely a department head or division leader.

ROLES AND RESPONSIBILITIES SUMMARY

Defining roles and responsibilities is a multiple step process that begins with detailed decisions and activities and works up to naming names. It is a mistake to begin with names because the people, although well intentioned, may not have the organizational authority or clout to do what needs to get done. Those programs end up failing or need to be overhauled. Also, people are much more likely to participate in the program if they understand what they are being asked to do and why it is important. Now, would I bring a bunch of identified stakeholders into a conference room and show them row after row of a RACI matrix? Absolutely not. But you can turn the RACI matrices into workflows that we will look at in greater dealer in Chapter 9, Operating Procedures.

CHAPTER 9

Operating Procedures

RESULTS YOU CAN EXPECT WITHOUT OPERATING PROCEDURES

One of the first things people tend to do when they are assigned a role in a Data Governance program is ask questions like:

- How much time am I going to have to spend on this?
- When do we meet?
- How do I prepare for meetings?
- Who else will be there?
- Who is in charge of meeting preparation?
- What does the agenda look like?
- Do I have to do work in between meetings?

If you define how the program is going to operate, people will have an easier time committing and participating. And if they don't commit and participate, the program is off to a bad start. There might be differing opinions on the level of program engagement needed or different groups might choose to operate differently from each other. Such an approach then becomes chaotic for all participants.

OPERATING PROCEDURES

Defining operating procedures for each of the identified decision-making bodies is key in your program becoming operational. Operating procedures are a beginning, not an end. As the different groups begin to work together, they may want to change how they operate and should have the ability to update operating procedures.

If you are writing operating procedures, here are the sections I would be sure to include, depending on the body the operating procedures apply to. Remember some of these to-do's were accounted for during the RACI exercise as outlined in Chapter 8, Roles and Responsibilties.

- Standing Agenda
- Meeting Cadence
- Meeting Preparation
- Chairperson
- Prioritization

- Voting
- Intake
- Escalation
- Annual Review
- Quorum
- Meeting Minutes

The following section is a starting point for operating procedures aligned to the Data Governance organizational framework we have been using. Yours might differ because of the detailed roles and responsibilities exercise. As a reminder, here it is (Figure 9.1).

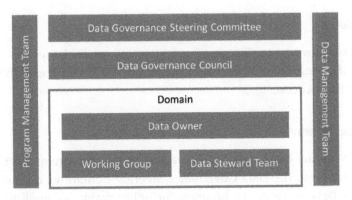

Figure 9.1 Data Governance Organizational Framework.

Data Governance Steering Committee

Standing Agenda

- Executive level briefing on key decisions
- Review any escalated issues
- Data Governance program status
- New requests
- Data Governance metrics
- Vote on appropriate items

Meeting Cadence

The Data Governance Steering Committee will meet on a quarterly basis.

Meeting Preparation

Program Management is responsible for distributing materials to the Data Governance Steering Committee members five business days before the meeting.

Prioritization

Annually, the Data Governance Steering Committee is responsible for the prioritization of Data Governance initiatives as reflected in the annual plan. There may also be regular updates to prioritization that require support/input from this committee.

Escalation

The Data Governance Steering Committee will resolve issues forwarded from the Data Governance Council in accordance with the established escalation process.

Annual Review

On an annual basis, Program Management will prepare an executive level report to the Data Governance Steering Committee on the state of the Data Governance program including major accomplishments and the vision for the coming year.

Meeting Minutes

Meeting minutes will be captured and published within two business days of the meeting. Minutes will include major discussion points and resulting decisions. The Program Management Team will capture and publish the minutes.

Data Governance Council

Standing Agenda

- Brief overview of program execution (roadmap/metrics)
- To-do list review (updated from last meeting)
- Decision check-in (policy/procedure review/approval)

- New issues
- Reviewing/updating DG assignments

Meeting Cadence

The Data Governance Council will meet for one hour on a monthly basis. The members may decide to change their cadence as the program matures.

Meeting Preparation

Program Management is responsible for distributing the agenda and any background materials to the Data Governance Council members five business days before the meeting.

Chairperson

The Data Governance Council will nominate and elect a Chairperson for the group on an annual basis. This individual will act as the point of contact for Data Governance activities.

Voting

A simple majority of the voting members in attendance is required for all decision approvals. The Chairperson has one additional vote when the council is evenly divided. If one of the council members wishes to appeal, they can submit new information to the Chairperson for consideration. The Chairperson can then make the decision to allow the Data Governance Council to take a second vote after considering the new information or escalate the issue to the Data Governance Steering Committee for their review.

Members are expected to attend and vote in person; proxy votes are not allowed.

Intake

Program Management will maintain a log of both open and closed Data Governance related issues. The Data Stewards, in collaboration with the

Data Owners, will assist those wishing to raise new issues. The Data Stewards assigned to the domain area should document the issue and assess initial solutions. New issues can originate from various sources and will be forwarded to Program Management to review, assess, and prioritize before being placed on the agenda for the Data Governance Council.

Escalation

In cases where the Data Governance Council is unable to reach a decision on an issue, the issue under consideration can be escalated to the Data Governance Steering Committee for resolution.

Annual Review

On an annual basis, Program Management will prepare a report for the Data Governance Council about the state of the Data Governance program including major accomplishments and the vision for the coming year.

Quorum

To reach a quorum, a minimum of 80% of the permanent voting members must be present.

Appeal

The first step when a Data Governance Council member wishes to appeal is to submit new information to the Chairperson. The Chairperson will then decide if a second council vote is warranted, or if the request should be forwarded to the Data Governance Steering Committee.

Meeting Minutes

Meeting minutes will be captured and published within two business days of the meeting. Minutes will include major discussion points and resulting decisions. The Program Management Team will be responsible for capturing and distributing meeting minutes.

Attendance

Members, representatives, and presenters are expected to attend meetings in person or via conference call/Teams meeting.

Data Owner

Standing Agenda

- New issue review
- To-do list review (updated from last meeting)
- Prioritization
- Assign working teams
- Domain policy review
- Reviewing/updating Data Steward and Working Group assignments

Meeting Organization

The Data Owner will meet on a regular basis with Working Groups and Data Stewards to review domain priorities, communicate activity status, coordinate domain activities, and identify items for the Data Governance Council meeting. The meeting cadence will be at the discretion of the Data Owner.

Intake

The Data Owner will review domain data related issues with the Data Stewards and Working Groups and forward them to the Data Governance Council as appropriate.

Data Steward Team

Standing Agenda

The Data Steward team will meet as needed or on a regular schedule as determined by the team or by the Data Owner.

- To-do list review
- Review of ongoing policy/procedure development

- New issues
- Review/update Data Steward assignments

Team Organization

Data steward team leads may be selected to represent individual topics or initiatives for the purpose of coordinating and communicating the outcomes to the Data Stewardship Team, the Data Owner, and/or the Data Governance Council.

Intake

The Data Steward Team is the point of contact for users wishing to submit domain data related issues to the Data Owner or Data Governance Council for review. The Data Steward Team will assist users in documenting the issue and potential impacts and identify possible solutions.

Working Group

Working Groups will meet on an ad-hoc basis or as required by the Data Owner. The Data Owner will make decisions on how these teams will function and communicate progress.

Program Management Team

Communications

- Publish reports
- Plan training based on education needs
- Maintain web-portal as appropriate
- Communication and interaction with the stakeholders

Support Data Governance Decision-Making Bodies

- Prepare agenda preparation and other materials, as necessary, for meeting

- Schedule and facilitate meeting
- Capture and distribute meeting minutes
- Meet/collaborate with the Data Stewards

Annual Review

On an annual basis, Program Management will conduct an overall assessment of the program. This assessment will include Data Governance metrics, processes, tools, training needs, staffing needs, and areas that will need focus/improvement for the coming year.

Data Management Team

The Data Management Team will be represented on the Data Governance Council and will interact with the other decision-making bodies as needed. The team will determine their cadence for meeting regularly and reporting progress.

A SIMPLIFIED VIEW OF OPERATING PROCEDURES

While it is important to document how the program needs to work, a lot of what you just read is intended to handle exceptions. I have not been in an organization where the Data Governance Steering Committee is spending time addressing issues that cannot be resolved at the Data Governance Council or Data Owner level. One of the reasons for defining the organizational structure is to encourage and empower decision making at the lowest level that makes sense for the data and the organization.

As you design your program, think about the exceptions but more importantly, determine what the participants need to know in the short term to become operational. Those are the most important things to communicate, and that can be done with the following picture that defines operating procedures for members of the Data Governance Council (Figure 9.2).

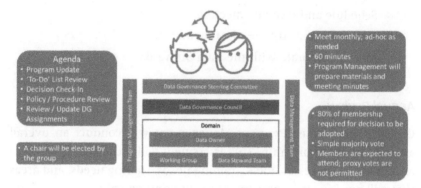

Figure 9.2 Data Governance Council Operating Procedures.

Looking at the picture, members can easily understand they will be expected to meet once per month and perhaps more if circumstances arise. They know there is a standing agenda and that the Program Manager will handle those details. One of them will be the chairperson. Lastly, 80% will need to attend if a simple majority decision is required and they cannot send delegates.

WORKFLOWS

Another great tool for communicating operating procedures is through creating workflows for key activities. Workflows are a great means for showing the results of the RACI model exercise in terms of an operating process. I am not suggesting you need to draw a workflow for each and every line item in the list of key activities and decisions. I am, however, suggesting you choose some of the most important activities for the Data Governance program and represent them in terms of a workflow. I typically start with a group of four: policy development, data issue intake, compliance monitoring, and prioritization.

Policy Development

This is one of the first tasks participants will be asked to engage in as the program becomes operational. Here are the details from the RACI model for data quality policy development (Table 9.1).

Table 9.1 Policy Development RACI.

Activities	PM	DGSC	DGC	DO	WG	DS	DM
Create data quality policy	C	I	A	R	R	R	R
Approve data quality policy	C	I	A	R	R	I	I
Publish data quality policy	R	I	A	I	I	I	I

Here is that representation in a workflow (Figure 9.3).

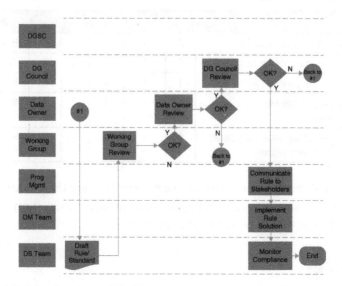

Figure 9.3 Policy Development Workflow.

You can follow the responsibilities of each group much easier in the workflow than in the RACI matrix, although it serves as a reference for the workflow development. The workflow clearly shows that the Data Owner begins the process and assigns work to the Data Steward Team to draft the policy. The Working Group also has responsibility for approval so there is a review step there before approval by the Data Owner. Once that approval is granted, the policy would then move to the Data Governance Council to become an official policy as it is that group that has final accountability for policy creation, development, and approval. Once the policy has final approval, it then is up to Program Management to communicate, Data Management to implement the solution (if necessary and remember, an IT project may be required to accomplish it), and finally for the Data Stewards to monitor against the policy outcome.

Data Issue Intake

As soon as stakeholders understand there is a Data Governance program, they want to get their particular challenge addressed. Not every issue you hear about is going to be one that Data Governance can fix. Because of this, there needs to be a defined process for gathering requests and deciding which ones to address (Table 9.2).

Table 9.2 Data Issue Intake RACI.

Activities	PM	DGSC	DGC	DO	WG	DS	DM
Maintain consolidated issue list	A	I	I	R	R	R	R
Facilitate communication across domains	A	I	R	R	R	C	R
Remediate data quality issues	I	I	A	C	R	R	R
Identify and prioritize key data to be monitored	I	I	A	R	I	R	C
Identify data quality issues, root causes, and proposed remediation	I	I	A	R	R	R	C

Each of the activities listed above help in defining the workflow for reviewing, assigning, assessing, and determining a remediation path as shown in the workflow below (Figure 9.4).

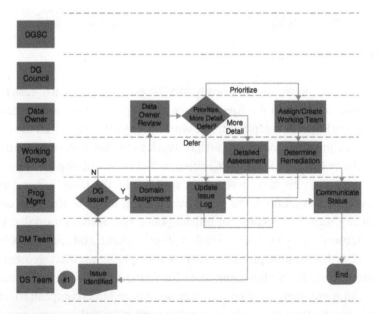

Figure 9.4 Data Issue Intake Workflow.

In our roles and responsibilities exercise, we defined the Data Stewards as a central point of contact for data issues, so that team is the starting point of the workflow. The Data Stewards will work with Program Management to determine if the issue is appropriate to be addressed by the Data Governance Organization. If so, it will be assigned to a specific domain. The Data Owner will then have the ability to defer, prioritize, or ask for more detail to be provided. If the issue is deferred, the log is updated, and the status communicated to the requestor. If the Data Owner chooses to prioritize and address the issue, they may establish a Working Group team to address and determine remediation (remember, Data Stewards may or may not be part of a Working Group). Finally, if the Data Owner needs more information, they may assign the issue to a Working Group to complete a more detailed assessment before a decision can be made. Regardless of the path, Program Management will maintain the issue log and facilitate communication across stakeholder groups.

Compliance Monitoring

As policies are developed, it is important to understand what it means to be compliant with said policies. If there is no measurement, compliance becomes a courtesy and not a requirement. Compliance might not happen overnight, but it still needs to be measured. Table 9.3 lists the RACI activities regarding policy compliance.

Table 9.3 Compliance Monitoring RACI.

Activities	PM	DGSC	DGC	DO	WG	DS	DM
Communicate policy compliance and progress	R	I	A	C	I	R	I
Monitor compliance with policies	C	I	A	R	R	R	R
Grant policy compliance waiver	I	I	A	R	C	C	C

The workflow is the outcome of those activities including monitoring, deciding courses of action for non-compliance, and communicating to stakeholders (Figure 9.5).

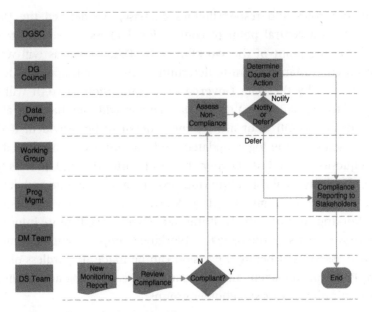

Figure 9.5 Compliance Monitoring Workflow.

Responsibility for compliance monitoring falls on the Data Stewards. An example might be ensuring metadata has been collected and the repository updated for a new data subject area. If the metadata exists, the Data Steward would report that to Program Management. If not, the Data Owner for the appropriate data domain would be notified. The Data Owner can then make a determination if a waiver is to be granted or if the Data Governance Council needs to be notified and help determine the course of action. Either way, compliance reporting will be a function of Program Management.

Prioritization

It is important for the Data Governance program to focus on the most important business data challenges. It is the role of executive leadership to ensure direction is set for Data Governance along with all the other strategic initiatives for the organization. After that, it is the role of the Data Governance Council to align Data Governance priorities to overall organizational priorities (Table 9.4).

Table 9.4 Prioritization RACI.

Activities	PM	DGSC	DGC	DO	WG	DS	DM
Set strategic direction and goals for Data Governance	C	A	R	R	C	I	I
Set Data Governance priorities	C	C	A	R	I	C	C

Here is the workflow for prioritization that also reflects Data Governance activities, which come from multiple sources including executive leadership, the issue list, and IT project delivery (Figure 9.6).

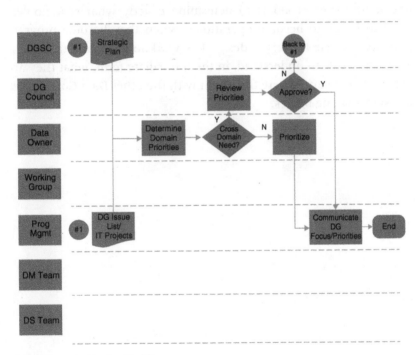

Figure 9.6 Prioritization Workflow.

The Data Governance Steering Committee maintains the alignment to overall strategies, and Program Management maintains alignment to the Data Governance issue list and any IT projects requiring Data Governance support. From those two inputs, the Data Owner will determine the priorities within the domain. If there is a cross-domain need, the Data Governance Council will help set priorities. If not, the Data Owner will determine their domain priorities. Program Management then communicates Data Governance priorities to the stakeholders.

OPERATING PROCEDURES SUMMARY

It is important to define operating procedures so that program participants understand their commitment and how the program is going to function. The ways to do this are three-fold. The first is to formally document. The second is to determine exactly what stakeholders need to know to become operational when they become program participants. The third is to design key workflows. Again, the goal is for participants to understand, in the immediate term, what they are expected to do and where they fit in with the other Data Governance decision-making bodies.

CHAPTER **10**
Communication

RESULTS YOU CAN EXPECT WITHOUT COMMUNICATION

Two things happen when a Data Governance program kicks off. The first is a level of excitement from the people who have put forth the effort to get the program off the ground. The second is reluctance from stakeholders about participation and what the program is meant to accomplish. You need to build a communication strategy that keeps the momentum and excitement going while ensuring stakeholders understand what Data Governance is supposed to achieve and how the organization is progressing toward meeting objectives. You do this through communication. If you fail to communicate, the momentum will decrease and reluctance, all the way to non-participation, will increase.

COMMUNICATION PLAN COMPONENTS

From the Data Governance program outset, as it is being established and then as implementation begins, end users (including individuals not actively involved in the program) need to be informed on the intent and goals of the Data Governance program and how they align to the overall objectives for the organization. This is key to generating awareness, maintaining transparency, and promoting the value of Data Governance processes.

Communication needs to be thought through with as much diligence as the creation of the organizational framework. Every organization has communication mechanisms in place, whether it is mass e-mails, intranet, or posters in the break room. Regardless of how messages or material are shared, there needs to be a formal communications strategy that, at minimum, identifies the list below.

Message

The message is essentially the overarching title and the description of what is going to be communicated. When it comes to communications, there are many categories. I like to group them into buckets for organization. Those categories include the following (Table 10.1).

Table 10.1 Prioritization RACI.

Communication Category	Purpose
Program Orientation	• Introduce basic concepts of Data Governance • Differentiate Data Governance and Data Management activities • Address gaps identified from stakeholder survey results • Illustrate business value of Data Governance and benefits of shared data
Program Design	• Create foundational materials that define the purpose and intent of the Data Governance program • Promote understanding of Data Governance in practice • Obtain executive support for further Data Governance program design
Tools and Templates	• Provide standard templates to simplify and standardize documentation • Support Data Stewards in their daily work • Promote consistency across departments and domains
Training	• Educate stakeholders of the Data Governance program • Train participants in how to engage in Data Governance • Support adoption of Data Governance processes
Program Metrics and Reports	• Establish measures to track progress of DG program • Validate the benefits of Data Governance by measuring project parameters • Develop standardized reports to share with stakeholders and executive leadership to monitor progress and communicate

Objective

Some communications might contain updates, some might be a request for approvals. Regardless of the expected outcome, each communication should have a stated purpose in terms of what the intended audience will receive as well as any actions the audience is expected to take.

Author(s)

Somebody has to be responsible for the creation and maintenance of each communication. Some of the communication responsibilities were already identified during the RACI exercise. For example, the

Data Governance Program Manager is not responsible for creating and approving policies but owns the process of publishing and communicating policies to the broader organization.

Audience

Each communication is received and consumed by a target audience. In addition to the different Data Governance participants, other recipients may include department heads, human resources, legal, IT development teams, and project managers.

Frequency

Communication needs to have a defined cadence. Most importantly, the cadence needs to be regular. If you tell executives you are going to send a quarterly update, you send them a quarterly update on time.

Medium

There are many options for distributing or sharing communication. These might include a SharePoint site, company intranet, external website, e-mail, newsletters, training sessions, in-person meetings, and self-service reports. Communication vehicles are dependent on how the organization is used to receiving information and the utilization of readily available tools.

SAMPLE COMMUNICATION PLAN

The following table describes key program communications. The initial plan does not need to be locked in place forever. A communication plan should be a flexible and ongoing framework for facilitating awareness, adoption, and participation in the Data Governance program. Therefore, additional persistent and as-needed communication mechanisms are expected to be added as the program matures. Such additions will capture formal interactions with other business and IT groups as they are solidified as well as addressing requirements to support increasing scope and entrenchment of Data Governance over time (Table 10.2).

Table 10.2 Data Governance Communication Plan.

Message	Objective	Author	Audience	Frequency	Medium
Data Governance Organization Strategy	Communicate alignment of Data Governance resources, funding, and activities to strategic roadmap and planned initiatives	Program Management	• All	Program Initiation/Annual	Online/Newsletter
Data Governance Program Roadmap	Articulate key initiatives, milestones, and status; promote awareness and engagement in Data Governance	Program Management	• All	Program Initiation/Annual	Online/Newsletter
Data Governance Program Scorecard and Update	Demonstrate Data Governance program status/progress toward objectives, program compliance, achievements, tracking toward objectives, and areas for improvement	Program Management	• All	Quarterly	Online/Newsletter
Data Governance Issue Intake Request	Capture issues for Data Governance consideration	Program Management	• Data Owner Team • Data Stewards • Stakeholders	Ongoing	Online template
Data Owner Team Meeting Agenda	Communicate planned meeting issues and status; provide pre-meeting materials to address	Program Management	• Data Owner Team	Per Meeting Frequency	Online
Data Owner Meeting Minutes	Document issues addressed, decisions made, pending actions	Program Management	• Data Owner Team	Per Meeting Frequency	Online

(Continued)

157

Table 10.2 *(Continued)*

Message	Objective	Author	Audience	Frequency	Medium
Data Steward Agenda	Communicate planned meeting issues and status; provide pre-meeting materials to address	Meeting Chair	▪ Program Management ▪ Data Stewards ▪ Data Owner Team ▪ Stakeholders	Per Meeting Frequency	Online
Data Steward Meeting Minutes	Document issues addressed, decisions made, pending actions	Meeting Chair	▪ Program Management ▪ Data Stewards ▪ Data Owner Team ▪ Stakeholders	Per Meeting Frequency	Online
Steering Committee Agenda	Communicate planned meeting issues and status; provide pre-meeting materials to address	Program Management	▪ Data Governance Steering Committee ▪ Data Owner Team ▪ Stakeholders	Per Meeting Frequency	Online
Steering Committee Team Minutes	Document issues addressed, decisions made, pending actions	Program Management	▪ Data Governance Steering Committee ▪ Data Owner Team ▪ Stakeholders	Per Meeting Frequency	Online
Data Governance Charter	Establish the mission, objectives, and framework for the Data Governance program	Program Management/Data Owner Team	▪ All	Initiation/ Updated as Necessary	Online
Published Data Governance Policies and Standards	Raise awareness of approved Data Governance policies for adoption among stakeholder groups	Program Management	▪ All	Ongoing	Online

Table 10.2 (*Continued*)

Message	Objective	Author	Audience	Frequency	Medium
Data Governance Operating Procedures	Educate participants on defined processes and methods for engaging with the Data Governance program	Program Management	▪ Data Owner Team ▪ Data Stewards ▪ Stakeholders	Initiation/Updated as Necessary	Online
Data Governance Templates	Provide tools for stakeholders to engage with Data Governance teams	Program Management	▪ Data Stewards ▪ Stakeholders	Initiation/Updated as Necessary	Online
Training Materials	Provide targeted education to stakeholders, Data Stewards, and Data Owner members on Data Governance processes	Program Management	▪ Data Owner Team ▪ Data Stewards ▪ Stakeholders	Initiation/Updated as Necessary	Online/In-person

COMMUNICATION SUMMARY

Communication is important to the sustainability of the Data Governance program and is one of the key responsibilities of the Program Management function. Rolling out the communication plan will not happen all at once. If your program is new, there is quite a bit of collateral to develop and distribute. Be thoughtful. I like to think about developing program collateral "just in time" for when you will need it. Plan for the time it will take, review with key stakeholders, and deliver to stakeholders as they need it. If you send everything out in one big package, stakeholders will feel overwhelmed and that will lead to reluctance to participate. Think about what communication methods already work in your organization and leverage them first. Do not be nervous if you need to adjust over time. Most importantly, stick to the plan as you have designed it. The worst ball to drop is the one about letting people know where they fit into Data Governance and how the program is supporting overall business objectives.

CHAPTER 11

Measurement

RESULTS YOU CAN EXPECT WITHOUT MEASUREMENT

Measurement is important. If your organization is committing time and resources to a Data Governance program, you need to be committed to measuring progress. If you do not, interest will wane and you will be at risk of losing executive support over time.

WHAT MEASUREMENTS TO DEFINE

A fundamental practice in support of successful Data Governance is developing metrics that communicate the activities and value of the program. Measures should reflect the major activities (policy development, issue identification and resolution, quality improvements, and participation by involved stakeholders, etc.) ongoing in the Data Governance program. They can change over time but should promote the multifaceted value provided by formalizing Data Governance practices for a broad set of data stakeholders.

At the start of the Data Governance program, baseline metrics (where appropriate) should be collected to measure against. Things like improvements in data quality, more complete data definitions, or time to issue resolution should be tracked in order to demonstrate improvements to end users. As the program matures, you may be able to publish a Data Governance program scorecard with standard metrics that are communicated on a regular basis. This is an important means of sustaining transparency of the Data Governance program (Table 11.1).

Table 11.1 Sample Data Governance Program Measures.

Objective: Establish an organizational framework with clear roles and responsibilities that enable sustainable execution across multiple domains		
Goal	**Measure**	**Indicator(s)**
Data Governance is established, and members are actively participating in governance processes	Meeting attendance and participation	• Meeting attendance (trend) • % of meetings in which quorum is achieved
	Data Governance servicing multiple domains	• Number of domains that Data Governance supports
	Decisions made	• Number of decisions made • Number of policies approved
Organization is compliant with data policies and standards	Compliance measured against thresholds as specified in the policy or standard, which will vary Examples might include: • Metadata standards • Data quality standards • Data usage policies	• % of policies where compliance is met • % of policies with partial compliance
Data Governance roles are defined so that Data Governance participants and business stakeholders understand the execution process	Milestone activities completed on-time (per the Program Roadmap)	• % of milestone dates are achieved
	Roles approved and filled	• # of roles filled for Data Owners and Data Steward Team(s)
	Demand for Data Steward support across projects	• % milestone dates are met • Capacity of Data Stewards available to support projects
	Delivery of training for Data Governance program: • Tools • Processes	• % target dates met per roadmap; will require ongoing review and refinement as part of overall program management function
Establish key operating processes and procedures	Formalization of key operating procedures per Business Data Roadmap: • Program Charter • Communication Plan • Data Governance Operating Procedures • Other • Training material	• Completion and status relative to defined completion date • Approval and adoption by Data Owners

(Continued)

Table 11.1 *(Continued)*

Goal	Measure	Indicator(s)
Data Owner role established and operational	Authorization and approval for DO and initiation of DO activities	▪ Data Owner members approved by DGSC ▪ Data Owner meetings initiated
Objective: Ensure core data domains are integrated into single versions to support reporting/analytic needs across departments		
Goal	Measure	Indicator(s)
Realize business value of eliminating redundant or conflicting business processes and practices	Business value will be measured against defined Data Governance policy or project objectives. These may not be able to be defined until use cases for integrated data are implemented. Some examples: ▪ Increased productivity or time to complete key business process (e.g., reduce time to onboard a new product or vendor) ▪ Reduction in redundant data sources or storage points; cost avoidance due to reusing existing assets ▪ Reduced solution delivery time for business process and/or application changes ▪ Reduced costs due to redundant processes	▪ TBD* ▪ Actual vs. Target Value* *Note*: May be measured in #, %, red/green/yellow depending on specific policy or standard
Objective: Increase the overall trust in data through implementation of a data quality process		
Goal	Measure	Indicator(s)
Measure data quality of key data and share results with stakeholders	Is data quality of a data store acceptable?	▪ Number of fields/terms included in data quality service level agreements (SLA) ▪ % of fields where data quality meets the requirements in the SLA
	Are data quality measures defined?	▪ % of terms with data quality metrics

Table 11.1 (*Continued*)

Objective: Establish a metadata process to ensure business rules, policies, documents, and news are accessible and searchable across departments		
Goal	**Measure**	**Indicator(s)**
Business terms are consistently defined	Definitions are documented	▪ % of terms that are fully updated in the metadata repository
Build searchable metadata repository and promote its use across departments	▪ Does a metadata repository exist? ▪ Are teams aware and accessing the repository on a regular basis?	▪ Existence of a metadata repository ▪ % of terms included ▪ Survey of awareness
Objective: Generate awareness around the use of the data, its value, and the need for governance		
Goal	**Measure**	**Indicator(s)**
Establish and communicate known authority and accountability for Data Governance	Execute against Communication Plan	▪ Communication Plan milestones met
Objective: Assign clear authority and accountability for data assets		
Goal	**Measure**	**Indicator(s)**
Establish and communicate known authority and accountability for Data Governance	Identify data owners	▪ % of terms in data dictionary with assigned data owners
Objective: Maintain a consistent definition of the data and its business rules		
Goal	**Measure**	**Indicator(s)**
Business terms are consistently defined	Definitions are documented	▪ % of terms that are fully updated in the metadata repository
Issues are addressed at the appropriate level of the Data Governance organization	Frequency of issue escalation	▪ % Issues Escalated (from Data Owners to DGSC or Data Steward Team to Data Owners) – Trend Note: Upward trend may indicate inability of Data Owners to come to consensus or discomfort in making and owning decisions – action may be required

(*Continued*)

Table 11.1 (*Continued*)

Goal	Measure	Indicator(s)
	Frequency of rejected issues	▪ % Issues Rejected (from Data Owners to Data Steward Team; or Data Owners/Data Stewards to Submitter) – Trend Note: Upward trend may indicate Data Owner's desire to push decision making down in the organization
Objective: Eliminate redundant or conflicting business processes and practices		
Goal	**Measure**	**Indicator(s)**
Realize business value of eliminating redundant or conflicting business processes and practices	Business value will be measured against defined DG policy or project objectives. For example: ▪ Increased productivity or time to complete key business process (e.g., reduce time to onboard a new product or vendor) ▪ Reduction in redundant data sources or storage points; cost avoidance due to reusing existing assets ▪ Lower time to market for business process and/or application changes ▪ Reduce costs due to redundant processes	▪ TBD* ▪ Actual vs. Target Value* *Note*: May be measured in #, %, red/green/yellow depending on specific policy or standard

PROGRAM SCORECARD – A STARTING POINT

I am not suggesting that each of these measures needs to be tracked from the first day of the Data Governance program. They need to follow along with the roadmap. I recommend a simple scorecard that measures participation, program establishment, and compliance to initial policies. Here are the examples and why they are important.

Data Governance Participation

The simplest way to measure program participation is through attendance at working sessions. The key decision-making body, the Data Governance Council in our examples, is the best place to start. Our operating procedures told us that 80% of the membership was required to make any decisions, so 80% is the threshold. Here is a simple attendance chart (Table 11.2). A "1" means the participant was present, a "0" means they were absent.

Table 11.2 Data Governance Council Meeting Attendance.

Date	Total	Participation	Mary Anne	Faramarz	Matthias	Matt	Katie	Liz	Noah	Robert	Patrick	Bryan
			6	7	7	6	6	7	7	6	3	7
			86%	100%	100%	86%	86%	100%	100%	86%	43%	100%
Jan	10	100%	1	1	1	1	1	1	1	1	1	1
Feb	10	100%	1	1	1	1	1	1	1	1	1	1
Mar	9	90%	1	1	1	1	1	1	1	1	0	1
Apr	7	70%	1	1	1	0	0	1	1	1	0	1
May	9	90%	1	1	1	1	1	1	1	1	0	1
Jun	9	90%	1	1	1	1	1	1	1	0	1	1
Jul	8	80%	0	1	1	1	1	1	1	1	0	1

A quick glance at the chart shows the group is generally meeting the 80% attendance goal. I would question why Patrick was not in attendance between March and May. The reasons could be that Patrick does not feel he has the time or does not see the value in participation. Whatever the reason, the attendance shows he is not actively participating. Also, the team would not have been allowed to make any decisions in April because they did not have a quorum. Participation under that 80% mark means the progress of the entire program can be hindered. This can easily be transformed into a graph that shows attendance over time (Figure 11.1).

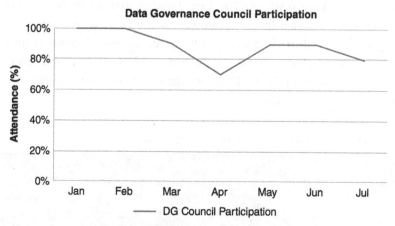

Figure 11.1 Data Governance Council Meeting Participation.

What if the attendance looked more like the following attendance chart (Table 11.3)?

Table 11.3 Data Governance Council Meeting Attendance.

Date	Total	Participation	Mary Anne	Faramarz	Matthias	Matt	Katie	Liz	Noah	Robert	Patrick	Bryan
			4	5	3	6	4	6	7	6	3	7
			57%	71%	43%	86%	57%	86%	100%	86%	43%	100%
Jan	10	100%	1	1	1	1	1	1	1	1	1	1
Feb	9	90%	0	1	1	1	1	1	1	1	1	1
Mar	8	80%	1	1	0	1	1	1	1	1	0	1
Apr	6	60%	1	1	0	0	0	1	1	1	0	1
May	5	50%	0	0	0	1	0	1	1	1	0	1
Jun	8	80%	1	1	1	1	1	0	1	0	1	1
Jul	5	50%	0	0	0	1	0	1	1	1	0	1

It is not just Patrick in this example not showing up. With the exception of Noah and Bryan, attendance appears to be getting weaker as the months go by (Figure 11.2).

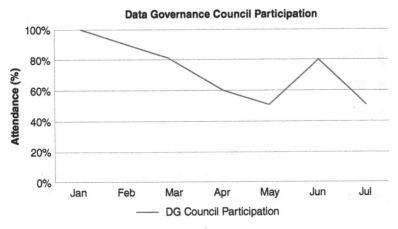

Figure 11.2 Data Governance Council Meeting Participation.

This trend shows a program that is faltering. March or April would be a good time for Program Management to step in to assess why participation is consistently under the 80% threshold. Just like with the example of Patrick above, maybe people are not allowed the time to participate, they do not see the value Data Governance is providing, or they do not feel empowered to make decisions. Regardless of the root cause(s), months have gone by without the ability to make formal decisions, and that should be addressed.

Data Governance Program Milestones

We are going to dedicate an entire chapter (Chapter 12, Roadmap) to developing a program roadmap so specifics here are not necessary. However, when defining a roadmap and adding a timeline, you are creating a mechanism for measuring the progress of your program. How granular you want to get is dependent on your organization. My recommendation is to break down the milestones by the swim lanes in the roadmap. Here is a simple example that breaks the milestones down into program management and policy development (Figure 11.3).

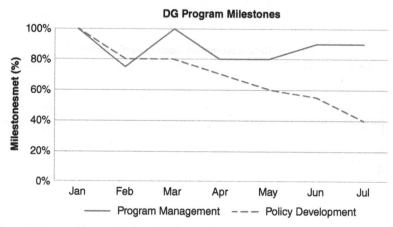

Figure 11.3 Data Governance Program Milestones.

The data points tell two stories. One is that the program management milestones are generally being met so the program is moving forward. On the other hand, policy development is lagging. The March/April time frame would be a good time to assess why policies are not making it through the development process. Are the right people not involved? Can the teams not come to agreement? Is the final approval process too arduous? Was the timeline too aggressive? Are policies stalled because there is no technology in place to support the needs? There could be more reasons. This might be a time to escalate to leadership or to reassess the roadmap timeline.

Policy Compliance

Compliance to policy is something that is defined in the policy itself. There will be two sample policies in the Policies chapter. This part of the scorecard is measuring compliance to approved policies for metadata and data quality. Program Management will likely have to work with Data Owners and Data Stewards to collect data for this information.

Table 11.4 below is a starting point for the number of data elements over time in the environment. There were also high-impact elements that required a different level of governance (again, this is something that will be defined through policy).

Table 11.4 Data Governance Compliance Tracking.

Identified Data Elements	Jan	Feb	Mar	Apr	May	Jun	Jul
High-Impact Elements	12	30	60	65	70	90	150
Total Data Elements	130	200	350	475	600	650	825
Metadata Compliance	12	25	45	65	70	85	105
Data Quality Compliance	10	15	40	50	70	80	90

Here are the compliance calculations. Table 11.5 shows the percentage of identified high-impact data elements along with compliance to the policies. Compliance to metadata policy might mean terms are defined, metadata is collected, updated, and published. Data quality might mean data has been profiled, a baseline established, business rules defined, and compliance to rules is actively monitored. These are the types of callouts you would find in the policy.

Table 11.5 Data Governance Compliance Tracking by High-Impact Elements.

Identified Data Elements	Jan	Feb	Mar	Apr	May	Jun	Jul
High-Impact Elements	9%	15%	17%	14%	12%	14%	18%
Metadata Compliance	100%	83%	75%	100%	100%	94%	70%
Data Quality Compliance	83%	50%	67%	77%	100%	89%	60%

Looking at the graph for compliance, I would expect Program Management to question why there are drop-offs in July for both metadata and data quality. Because the number of governed data elements is growing, this could be an indicator that more staff or more sophisticated automation is needed to keep up with demand (Figure 11.4).

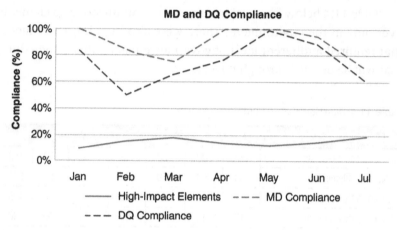

Figure 11.4 Data Governance Policy Compliance.

PROGRAM SCORECARD SAMPLE

We have now defined three sections of a scorecard that measure participation, progress, and compliance. With an area for updates, you have a report that is ready to be distributed. Most of the responsibility for getting information into the scorecard will fall on the shoulders of the Program Manager and they in turn will need to rely on input from program participants (Figure 11.5).

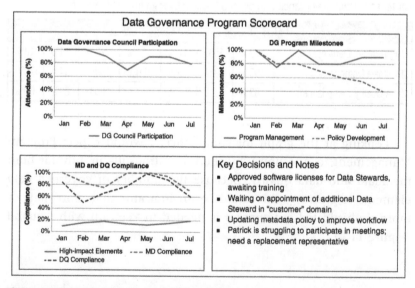

Figure 11.5 Sample Data Governance Scorecard.

MEASUREMENT SUMMARY

You do not need to start from scratch when thinking about how to measure the Data Governance program. Start with the objectives you have defined. If you have not yet identified objectives, do that first. While it might feel like a somewhat tedious exercise, it is vital to the ongoing sustainability of the program. People are more likely to participate if they understand what is being measured and who is looking at the reports. Case in point, Patrick is much more likely to attend Data Governance Council meetings if he knows his manager is on the distribution list.

CHAPTER **12**
Roadmap

RESULTS YOU CAN EXPECT WITHOUT A ROADMAP

Successful Data Governance programs have a common denominator, and that is people take the time to define activities and design the organizational structure that supports clear objectives. If you do not plan how to implement the organizational framework, you may end up with a program that is disorganized. Programs that start disorganized fall apart because the people get confused about what they are supposed to do and when they are supposed to do it. Programs that do not have a plan also do not have a way to measure or communicate. Those programs also fall apart because if it was not important enough to write activities down on a timeline, people will not think it important enough to participate, so they will focus on their other daily priorities.

FIRST STEP IN DEFINING A ROADMAP: IMPLEMENTING YOUR FRAMEWORK

You have defined objectives. You have defined guiding principles. You have defined an organizational framework that aligns to your culture and can support your objectives. You have defined operating procedures. Now you need to think about how to implement the framework. In other words, the order in which you will establish the different groups. Figure 12.1 shows our organizational structure for reference.

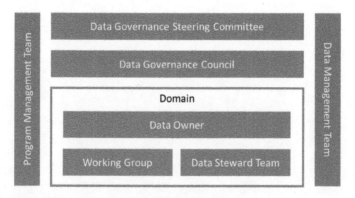

Figure 12.1 Data Governance Organizational Structure.

Things to consider when planning for the implementation order include maturity and readiness of program participants, existing processes or teams, and resource availability. Figure 12.2 is the implementation order for our example, along with how the order was determined.

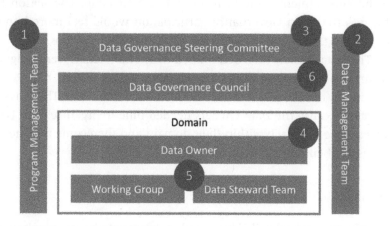

Figure 12.2 Implementation Order for Data Governance Organizational Structure.

The starting point was Program Management. This organization was starting from scratch and wanted to be sure to have all program collateral ready before onboarding the participants, particularly the Data Owners. There was also a formal job position created that was filled by one of the champions of Data Governance.

Formalizing the Data Management Team came next. This was a natural next step, as there was an existing informal data architecture team in place, but they were operating with no authority or coordination across projects. The Data Governance organizational framework gave the team a charter and a purpose. One of their first activities was the delivery of a data strategy, something that had been in development for quite some time.

An executive leadership team already existed, as is the case with most organizations. They set strategic direction for the organization and typically have regular interactions. In this organization, they added Data Governance requests and updates to their regular meeting cadence and became the Data Governance Steering Committee. Their first order of business was to formally appoint the domain Data

Owners. In organizations where executive support is unknown, this would likely be a first step.

Data Owners were identified for several key domains in support of a defined set of projects. The Data Owner team was implemented after the Data Governance Steering Committee because the messaging of the appointment came from executive leadership. The reason for this was that Data Governance participation would feel more important coming from senior leadership rather than peer groups.

The Data Owners then determined which individuals were assigned as part of a Working Group or appointed as Data Stewards.

Finally, the Data Governance Council was established. This was the last step because the Data Owners needed time to organize their Data Governance approach within their domain and then come together to represent their domain at the enterprise level.

DEFINING A ROADMAP

A roadmap is not a detailed project plan. It needs to have enough information that people can understand the to-dos of the program and have an idea of when activities are going to occur. That said, I always start with a "How to Read the Roadmap" picture so there is no question later what boxes, colors, timelines, or symbols mean (Figure 12.3).

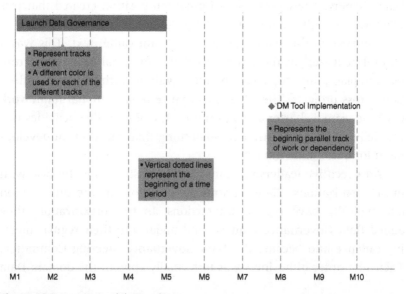

Figure 12.3 How to Read the Roadmap.

Workstreams

After deciding on the order of implementing the organizational frame-work, it is time to think about the activities. Creating swim lanes of activities is a great way to stay organized. Remember, you have already defined activities and decisions, so this step is taking those items and lay-ing them on a calendar. Our roadmap sample is broken down into six overall workstreams as shown in Figure 12.4. The six are Launch Data Governance, Data Warehouse Program Management, Data Architecture, Metadata, Data Quality, and Data Management. Launch Data Govern-ance was first to formalize the program. The Data Warehouse Program Management was intended to set data scope. Data Architecture was next to take advantage of the already-formed Data Management team. Meta-data and Data Quality were natural next steps, and then there was a step to address other Data Management challenges.

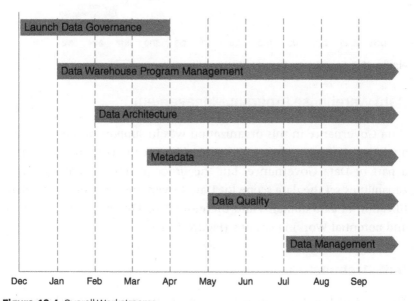

Figure 12.4 Overall Workstreams.

Launch Data Governance

Figure 12.5 shows the tasks associated with formalizing program roll-out. It includes finalizing the charter, communications plan, operating procedures, program metrics, workflows, and training material. This will enable participants to follow an established and formal process to conduct Data Governance activities. The onboarding order is reflective of the section above.

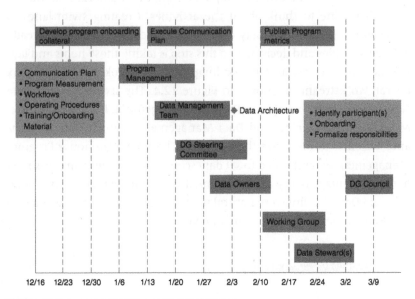

Figure 12.5 Launch Data Governance Workstream.

Data Warehouse Program Management

Data Governance in this organization was in support of reporting and analytics. Data Warehouse Program Management is not necessarily a part of Data Governance, but the order of reporting and analytic capabilities set the data scope for Data Governance as well as the identification of data domains and therefore Data Owners, Data Stewards, and potential Working Groups (Figure 12.6).

Data Architecture

The goal of this function is to establish an overall operational and analytic data architecture. The Data Architecture workstream begins with development of a conceptual data model that supports the identified reporting and analytic needs and definition of a data strategy. In this organization, it was understood that a tool implementation would be required to support data management activities such as data profiling, data quality, data integration, metadata, and data lineage.

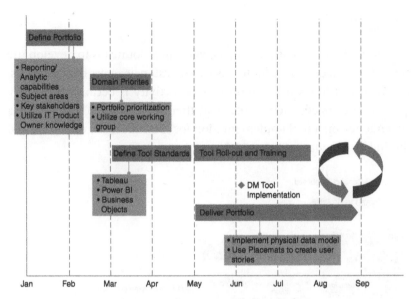

Figure 12.6 Data Warehouse Program Workstream.

The data strategy would identify those requirements. Data Architecture is also tasked with defining data integration and ETL standards (Figure 12.7).

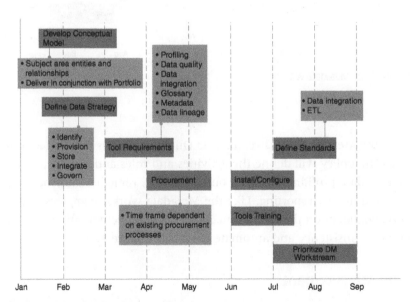

Figure 12.7 Data Architecture Workstream.

Metadata

One of the first tasks of the Data Governance Council is to develop the policy for Metadata in order to ensure consistency across data domains. The reason it looks like a months-long activity is because the policy is to be developed, then tested, and then formalized. There is also a dependency on a tool implementation for the collection, updating, and sharing of metadata (Figure 12.8).

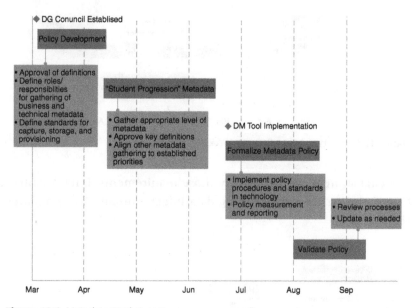

Figure 12.8 Metadata Workstream.

Data Quality

After the Metadata workstream, Data Quality becomes the next logical step. The policy will define the activities and roles and responsibilities such as data profiling, defining business rules, remediation processes, and data quality reporting. Like the Metadata workstream, this one is also dependent on the Data Management tool implementation to both provide consistency and automate processes (Figure 12.9).

Data Management

And finally, a Data Management workstream. In this organization, it was determined that the roadmap would be revisited to establish

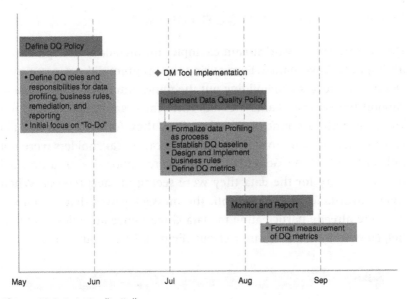

Figure 12.9 Data Quality Policy.

priorities once the data strategy and tool implementation tasks were completed (Figure 12.10).

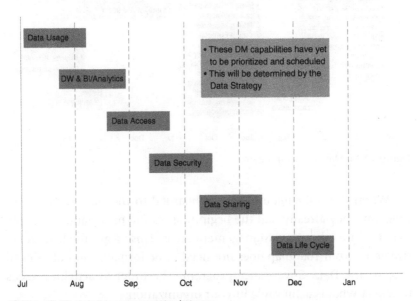

Figure 12.10 Data Management Workstream.

FORMALITY FIRST OR SAVE IT FOR LATER?

Here are two more workstream examples for metadata and operationalizing Data Governance. Formalizing the program did not come first. Defining a process and building out the minimum level of metadata to support reporting and analytics did. After the organization figured out what the right amount of metadata was, they formally started Data Governance. This approach was chosen because stakeholders were not onboard with "Data Governance" but were onboard with a detailed data dictionary for the data they were seeing in their reports. When Data Governance was kicked off, the messaging was that stakeholders were already participating in Data Governance activities, and that helped with formal program roll-out (Figures 12.11 and 12.12).

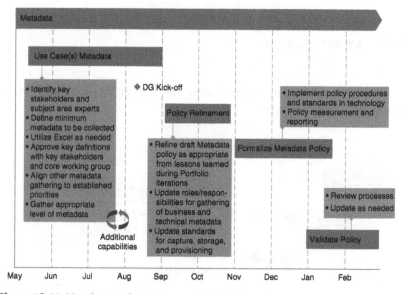

Figure 12.11 Metadata Workstream.

When the stakeholders were onboarded to the Data Governance program, they already had the beginnings of the policy and were able to move into other Data Management areas. This means the first workstream on your roadmap does not need to be formalization of roles to support the Data Governance program. The order of activities needs to reflect what is achievable in your organization.

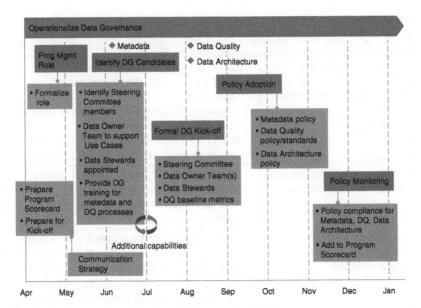

Figure 12.12 Operationalizing Data Governance Workstream.

CRITICAL SUCCESS FACTORS

Table 12.1 outlines some success factors that I share with all of my customers. These could also be re-worded as program risks. Keep them in mind as you build out your roadmap. If there are areas you think might need extra attention, be sure there is a call-out on the roadmap, so they are not forgotten.

Table 12.1 Data Governance Critical Success Factors.

Critical Success Factor	Description
Execution of communication plan	• Provide sponsors, key executives, and employees with regular updates on the program and report on success stories. This ensures continuous information flow and continued interest in the program as well as necessary funding. • Communicate that Data Governance is an on-going program – not a project.

(Continued)

Table 12.1 (*Continued*)

Critical Success Factor	Description
Continuous measurement of the benefits of the Data Governance program and related reports on a central accessible repository/portal	▪ Capture and report on metrics, which measure the program's impact on the organization on a regular basis. ▪ Improvements of data quality dimensions vs. baseline measures before the program. ▪ Number of key business terms that have been captured and defined with all necessary metadata attributes.
Adherence to the procedures and the standards of the program	▪ Monitor and ensure that old habits do not make their way back into common usage. ▪ Audit workflow compliance for data issue intake and reporting.
Measures for the program itself are captured and followed over time	▪ It is very important that the program itself is measured. That is the only way to objectively measure adoption, participation, and execution The Data Governance Program Management Team or a project management office are good candidates to implement and execute measurements.
Continuous execution of the training plan	▪ Inform and train new employees about their role in the Data Governance program. Allow enough time for those new employees to get familiar with their level of authority and their responsibilities. ▪ If employees change positions or get promoted, allow them to grow into the new role and understand their new duties regarding the Data Governance program.
Current information and news about the Data Governance program is actively managed on the organization's intranet or other information sharing portal	▪ Intranet portal or SharePoint site serves as a central point for information lookup and updates of the program accessible by all employees. ▪ The information in the portal must be complete, precise, and up to date. ▪ The site might serve as the central storage for Data Governance program artifacts, which have to be posted in a timely way or updated.
Comprehensive procedures exist that are based on the sanctioned Data Governance policies	▪ Published procedures will ensure that policies are organization-wide and consistently executed. ▪ Establish Data Governance as a repeatable, core business practice based on policy and procedures. ▪ Educate and train employees on procedures,
Policies and procedures are reviewed and adjusted as needed	▪ New regulations and new unknown data demand continuous review and adjustment of current policies and procedures.

Table 12.1 (*Continued*)

Critical Success Factor	Description
Data issues are addressed and resolved and data-related decisions are made on the lowest level (level is a body in the organizational framework) possible	<ul><li>Decisions about data should be made by its responsible body or the individual. Decisions frequently pushed up the ladder indicate that processes are not working, or decision makers do not have the authority, expertise, and/or training to make the decision.</li><li>The sponsor and executives provide value via their support and funding, not through participation on solving data-related issues.</li></ul>
Data Stewards are involved in every data project across the organization	<ul><li>Make data steward activities part of the project life cycle and ensure their participation early on.</li><li>Build Data Governance "gates" into delivery project plans.</li></ul>
Data access policies and data management routines are created to provide added security.	<ul><li>Data must be protected from unauthorized use.</li><li>The Data Governance program sets the foundation for data sharing across the organization. This can cause an increased risk of inappropriate use or publication of data. An example is sharing customer data with third parties or agencies without having the needed data sharing agreements in place.</li><li>Develop data security policies, which should include:<ul><li>Guidance on when to apply data masking and data encryption.</li><li>Periodic review of user/role access capabilities.</li><li>Guidance on sharing customer data with external third parties.</li></ul></li></ul>
A central data dictionary and data glossary are designed and established	<ul><li>Implement organization-wide central data dictionary and data glossary, which defines data, its usability and classification, and other metadata attributes.</li></ul>
Cooperation is promoted with IT groups by creating service level agreements	<ul><li>Ensure technical resource readiness/capability.</li><li>IT cooperation and service level agreements increase the chances of a successful Data Governance program. IT staff are the experts on technical data domains and enable the automation of data management routines, which are necessary for speedy data processing.</li></ul>

ROADMAP SUMMARY

The roadmap gives you an execution plan. The roadmap gives you a way to measure the outcomes of your program. The roadmap gives you a communication tool with stakeholders. It helps hold those stakeholders accountable for activities and decisions. The roadmap gives you a timeline and the ability to course correct if necessary. In building the roadmap, you need to think about how best to roll out the organizational framework depending on your organization's unique culture and overall readiness.

CHAPTER 13

Policies

RESULTS YOU CAN EXPECT WITHOUT POLICIES

Policies are core to providing oversight for data management activities. If policies do not exist, the Data Governance program is an academic exercise at best. The people involved will apply their own processes, methodologies, and rules. People will not know who to ask questions of and fall back to the individuals who have always been able to help them, regardless of whether that was their responsibility. People will not understand where business rules exist and how they impact data, causing distrust in reporting results. There are plenty more examples, but you get it. You end up with a chaotic data environment, not Data Governance.

BREAKING DOWN A POLICY

There are several inputs and considerations when developing a Data Governance policy. They consist of the policy statement, procedures, standards, and identified best practices that become Data Management processes. The breakdown of each of these components is shown in Figure 13.1.

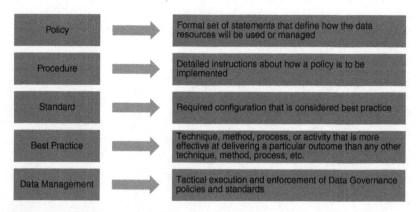

Figure 13.1 Components of a Policy.

Policy

A policy is a formal set of statements that define how the data resources will be used or managed. The statements should be as short and concise as possible so stakeholders will understand what is mandated. People also need to understand why the policy is important so there should be a stated policy objective that aligns to overall Data Governance program objectives. Policies can be broad in nature or granular. It depends on the situation at hand. An example of a broad policy might be one that applies across domains for metadata or data quality. A more granular policy might pertain to a product hierarchy in the product data domain.

Procedure

Procedures are the detailed instructions about how a policy is to be implemented. There may be one or several procedures that become an operating manual for a given policy. Like with operating procedures, some of these procedures had already been addressed when Data Governance activities and decisions were defined, and roles and responsibilities assigned. As such, the RACI matrix is a good place to start. For example, the following RACI matrix in Table 13.1 pertains to metadata.

Table 13.1 Metadata RACI Matrix.

Data Management Function	Activities	PM	DGSC	DGC	DO	WG	DS	DM
Metadata	Collect technical metadata	C	I	A	C	C	C	R
	Create business metadata	C	I	A	R	C	R	C
	Publish metadata	A	I	C	C	I	C	R
	Maintain metadata	C	I	A	R	C	R	C
	Maintain a searchable repository that is easily accessible by business stakeholders	I	I	A	R	I	R	R

The procedures would then define the process or checklist to follow when collecting technical metadata or creating business metadata.

Standard

Standards are the required configuration that is considered a best practice. Examples of standards can be data naming standards, security processes, defined hierarchies, or even which tools to use in what scenario. Standards need to be revisited and modified as technology advances or overall objectives change.

Best Practice

A best practice is a technique, method, process, or activity that is more effective at delivering a particular outcome than any other technique, process, activity, and so on. Best practices can be defined by management, industry experts, organizational consensus, or some combination of ideas that align to the organization's maturity and ability to work toward policy compliance.

Data Management

Data Management is the tactical execution and enforcement of Data Governance policies and standards. The goal of the Data Management function is to become compliant with policies because that compliance will in turn lead to more efficient practices that will create trusted and reusable data assets for the organization.

CONTENTS OF A POLICY

The following is a table of contents for development of a policy. Your organization might already have some type of template or required information for policies and procedures. If so, use that. If not, you can use this list as a starting point.

- Name
- Policy Purpose

- Policy Objectives
- Policy Statement
- Policy Details
- Attendant Procedures and Standards
- Scope/Affected Area(s)
- Roles and Responsibilities
- Compliance
- Effective Date
- Maintenance and Review

POLICY EXAMPLE – METADATA

The following is a policy example for metadata. This policy aligns to the objective we defined: "Establish a metadata process to ensure business rules, policies, documents, and updates are accessible and searchable across departments".

Name

Data Governance Metadata Policy

Policy Purpose

The purpose of the metadata policy is to provide enterprise directives for the collection, management, and publication of metadata and its application to data assets and services.

Policy Objectives

The objective of this policy is to support the use and reuse of information throughout the organization and enables the organization to know what data they have, where to find it, how to use it, and lays the foundation for eliminating multiple, contradictory versions of "the truth."

1. Provide an enterprise catalogue of the data and a common vocabulary

2. Improve data quality through better metadata

3. Improve business analytics and decision making through available metadata

4. Create data accountability by requiring data to be inventoried and documented

[Note how these policy objectives align to our overall program objectives. We are not trying to redefine the Data Governance objectives with policy development.]

Policy Statement

Relevant business and technical metadata for data objects will be collected and published via a metadata repository. The metadata will be updated and maintained to ensure its relevancy.

Metadata for the purpose of this policy is data that describes the business and technical characteristics of a data system, data source, data object, or data element. Metadata defines and gives value to a data asset.

[The actual policy statement is four sentences. The first two clearly state metadata will not only be collected and published but also kept up to date. The third and fourth sentences add some context by defining metadata and reiterating that it provides value to the asset.]

Policy Details

- Data Owners are accountable for submitting appropriate descriptive metadata for collection and storage in the metadata repository for the data within their domain. One or more Data Stewards must be assigned to ensure metadata procedures and standards are followed. Working Groups may also be utilized for adding business definitions and defining business rules.

- Data stores currently in operation will have key data elements designated and metadata defined for the key data elements based on business priorities. Priorities are aligned to the data that supports the reporting and analytic environment.

- The project delivery process will be modified so that metadata collection is part of every project that creates or uses data. This will ensure data is defined and inventoried in the development process as soon as possible and reduce downstream data quality and data integrity issues.
- A metadata repository will be developed and maintained to manage the metadata. Microsoft Excel is an acceptable starting point.
- Metadata will be easily available for searching and use by all data consumers.
- Compliance metrics, such as the number of new metadata definitions with minimal/full metadata definitions, will be collected and published.

[These policy details describe the policy at a more granular level. They refer to roles and responsibilities and other tasks that may have to be completed to support the policy. For example, the project delivery process needing to be updated. The details also state that there is no need to wait for a tool implementation because it is okay to get started with Microsoft Excel.]

Attendant Procedures and Standards

This policy requires that the Program Management Team publish operating procedures that outline specific activities that should be followed to comply with this policy.

- Business Metadata Standards and Procedures
- Technical Metadata Standards and Procedures
- Metadata Change Management Standards and Procedures
- Metadata Collection Standard Template

[The number of procedures referenced will be dependent on your organization. This policy required several because there were different teams associated with business and technical metadata collection. We do not need to reinvent roles and responsibilities for this step. Look back to the RACI matrix as a guide, and you will be able to develop workflows that are easy to follow.

Some organizations like procedures and standards to be in separate documents. If there are not that many, I like to include them all in one document because it is easier to manage.]

Metadata Collection Standard Template

The minimum set of metadata collected will be:

Data Dictionary	Description
Data Element Name	Business name of element
Description	Business description
Data Type	Physical data type (varies depending on database platform)
Valid Values	Valid data ranges; 1,0 for measures; valid date range
Source System	Source system database — may need to insert additional columns for multiple load "stops" (staging, DW --> DM)
Contact	Data Owner or Data Steward contact person

The recommended set of metadata collected will be:

Data Dictionary	Description
Subject Area	Subject area name or Grouping (dimensions)
Shared Entity	Entity or subject area
Data Element Name	Business name of element
Description	Business description
Alias/Report Label	Any other words or phrases that might be synonymous to data element name
Example Data	Sample data
Element Type	Simple — straight from source Calculated — transformed Key — used for look-up
Target System	Physical database name
Target Table Name	Physical table name
Target Field Name	Physical field name
Source System	Source system database — may need to insert additional columns for multiple load "stops" (staging, DW --> DM)
Source Table Name	Source system table name(s)
Source Field Name	Source system field names(s)

Data Dictionary	Description
Source Data Type	Physical data type in source system
Source Data Length	Number of digits and/or characters depending on data type
Transformation/ Load Rule	Transformation logic — pseudo code
Implementation Status	Existing — currently exists in the environment New — added by current initiative can be used for current project filtering
Attribute/Measure	Attribute — non-measures/dimensions Measure — fact measure Key — either primary or foreign
Sensitive Attribute	Y — sensitive data element (i.e., external enrollment, PII, etc.); N — not sensitive data
PII Attribute	Y — personally identifiable data element (i.e., SSN, name, address, etc.); N — not personally identifiable
Is PK?	Y — primary key; N — not primary key
Is FK?	Y — foreign key; N — not foreign key
FK Source	If a field is an FK, then the source system must be specified
Is NK?	Y — natural key; N — not natural key
Data Type	Physical data type (varies depending on database platform)
Length	Data element length
Null (Y/N)	Y — nullable; N — not nullable
Insert/Update	Insert — insert only; Update — update changes
Load Frequency	Daily, Weekly, Monthly, etc.
Valid Values	Valid data ranges; 1,0 for measures; valid date range
Data Governance Approval Status	Y — data element approved by data governance committee; N — not approved
Audit Process	Audit routine; NA means not audited
Comments	Open
Mapping to Consumers	This can be multiple columns — add each report, analysis query, or ad-hoc environment. This is useful to the business when they try and cross-reference an attribute to their "world."
Contact	Data Owner or Data Steward contact person
Last Updated By	Initials of person who last updated field
Date updated	Date updated

Scope/Affected Area(s)

All initiatives, applications, and projects creating, storing, moving, and using data that support the delivery of the reporting and analytics platform will be aligned with the Data Governance metadata policy and associated standards and procedures. This policy is applicable to all data stores that fall within this scope throughout the organization.

[This clearly states that any data associated with the reporting and analytics platform will be managed by this policy.]

Roles and Responsibilities

Data Steward

The Data Steward will aim to ensure the accuracy, usability, and accessibility of the metadata for their domain or focus area. They are responsible for:

- Working with Data Owners, business stakeholders, and subject matter experts to ensure metadata is collected and updated
- Reporting compliance metrics to Data Owner/Program Management

Data Management

Data Management will provide technical expertise regarding data assets and their associated metadata. They are responsible for:

- Administering the metadata repository and maintaining its integrity
- Collecting technical metadata

Program Management

The Program Management function will coordinate metadata processes across departments to promote collaboration, consistency, and communication. They are responsible for:

- Publishing metadata procedures and standards

- Ensuring the "quality" of the metadata submitted by Data Stewards and Data Owners in terms of meeting metadata standards
- Approving the publishing of metadata records

Data Owner

The Data Owner(s) will be accountable for implementing the policy within their domain focus area and submitting appropriate descriptive metadata for collection and storage in the metadata repository. Metadata status updates will be submitted to the Program Management team as needed.

[These statements outline responsibilities in enough detail that participants have a good idea of what they need to do to comply with the policy.]

Compliance

The Program Management function is accountable for auditing the process to evaluate compliance and the quality of metadata. The Data Stewards are responsible for following the metadata procedures and standards to ensure compliance with this policy. Compliance is defined as the existence and approval of the defined minimum level of metadata in the repository.

[These sentences define who monitors compliance and what it means to be compliant with the policy. It can be assumed that the scope of what data is required to have metadata has already been defined.]

Effective Date

This policy will be in force on the effective date of Xxx XX, 2023.

Maintenance and Review

Maintenance and review of this policy is set for 6 months after the initial release as indicated in the effective date. Subsequent review to this policy shall be based on a 12-month cycle.

[Policies need to be reviewed to determine if they need to be updated to reflect the "real world" scenarios of the program participants.]

POLICY EXAMPLE – DATA QUALITY

The following is a data quality policy example. This policy aligns to the objective we defined "Increase the overall trust in data through implementation of a data quality process."

Policy Purpose

The purpose of the data quality policy is to provide enterprise directives for a data quality process in support of Data Governance program objectives and delivery of the reporting and analytics platform.

Policy Objectives

The objective of this policy is to ensure the data quality strategy supports the trust and reuse of information across the various departments.

- Improve data quality
- Understand data quality baseline
- Define data quality
  - Thresholds
  - Action
  - Reporting dimensions
  - Service Level Agreements
- Define data quality measures
- Communicate data quality
- Reduce reoccurring data issues

Policy Statement

Data Owners will proactively assess, monitor, report, and improve data quality. For the purposes of this policy, data quality is defined as the conformance of data to the business definitions and the business rules (business metadata).

[This policy statement is two sentences long. There is a lot going on with the verbs, but this organization made the decision to consolidate all data quality into one overarching policy. For this organization, the most important word in the first sentence was "proactively." It made the statement that the organization

would no longer be in a reactionary or "firefighting" mode every time a data quality issue arose. The second sentence is simply a reminder of the definition of data quality.]

Policy Details

- Data Owners are accountable for defining their key data elements and creating a data quality monitoring and improvement plan for them. One or more Data Stewards must be assigned to governed domains to ensure data quality standards are being met.

- Data stores currently in operation will have key data elements designated and data quality acceptance levels defined for the key data elements based on business priorities.

- The project delivery process will be modified so that data quality assessment (profiling) is part of every project that creates or uses data. This will ensure data quality is defined as close to the data source as possible and monitored for compliance with established data quality acceptance levels.

- There will be documented procedures for reporting and correcting data quality issues with emphasis placed on identifying and eliminating data errors.

- Data quality issues and improvement metrics will be collected and published for each domain or focus area.

[These sentences reflect the details of the policy statement and begin to define some of the activities that will need to occur.]

Procedures

This policy requires published operating procedures that outline specific activities that should be followed to comply with this policy.

- The Data Stewards will evaluate the quality of the data in a specific focus area.

- The focus areas selected will be derived from the results of the prioritization process and focus on data that supports the reporting and analytic platform.

- The Data Steward will work with subject matter experts to establish data quality measures and remediation steps.

- Data Quality measures and thresholds will be included in the metadata repository for future reference.
- Program Management will collect and report standard data quality scorecards.
- The Program Management function will work with data producers and data consumers to establish Data Quality service level agreements.
- For data items found to have sub-optimal data quality, a new DG issue will be opened; the data owner will be notified and asked to submit a plan of action to close the compliance gap.

[This level of procedures was sufficient for this particular organization. Yours may require more detailed workflows or steps. If the list of procedures gets to be too long, I recommend moving to a separate document.]

Standards

A common set of tools will be used for data profiling, business rule development, remediation, and ongoing measurement.

[This organization was weary of different users writing different queries and then reporting on and remediating data quality issues. Creating this standard meant all data quality analysts and Data Stewards would use a common tool with centralized business rules and consistent reporting output.]

Scope/Affected Area(s)

All initiatives, applications, and projects creating, storing, moving, and using data that support the delivery of the reporting and analytic platform will be aligned with the Data Governance data quality policy and associated procedures and standards. This policy is applicable to all data stores that fall within this scope throughout the organization.

Roles and Responsibilities

Data Steward

The Data Steward will aim to ensure the quality and usability of the data for their data domain focus area. Data Stewards will work with Data Owners, business stakeholders, and subject matter experts to ensure data quality is improved and data issues are quickly resolved. They will be responsible for:

- Working with the Data Owner and business users to establish data quality metrics
- Helping define data quality acceptance levels
- Helping identify and remediate data issues within their domain
- Identifying and prioritizing data to be monitored and improved
- Ensuring the data within their domain meets the established data quality acceptance levels

Data Management

The Data Management team will work to implement a data quality tool set and work with Data Stewards to implement data quality business rules. They will be responsible for:

- Defining data quality business rules
- Implementing data quality business rules
- Establishing a data quality baseline
- Reporting and publishing data quality status
- Remediating data quality issues
- Identifying and recommending technology solutions to support the data quality process

Program Management

The Program Management function will coordinate data quality processes across departments to promote collaboration and communication. They will be responsible for:

- Defining consistent data quality measurement, remediation, and reporting procedures and standards
- Working with Data Owners, Data Stewards, and business users to establish data quality Service Level Agreements
- Collecting and publishing data quality metrics
- Reporting and publishing data quality status
- Monitoring and reporting compliance to the data quality policy

Data Owner

The Data Owner(s) will be accountable for implementing the data quality policy within their domain focus area and submitting appropriate data quality measurement and improvement plans. Data quality status reports will be submitted to the Program Management team as needed.

[These responsibilities came straight from the RACI matrix.]

Compliance

The Program Management function will ensure the procedures for measuring, correcting, and monitoring data quality are in place and meet the policy objectives. Compliance is achieved by:

- Having data profiled prior to movement and business rules applied
- Establishing a data quality baseline
- Defining data acceptance criteria
- Establishing processes for ongoing monitoring and remediation
- Communicating and publishing data quality results
- Establishing data quality service level agreements with data providers and consumers

Effective Date

This policy will be in force on the effective date of Xxx XX, 2023.

Maintenance and Review

Maintenance and review of this Policy are set for 6 months after the initial release as indicated in the effective date. Subsequent review to this Policy shall be based on a 12-month cycle.

POLICY SUMMARY

Defined policies are at the heart of the Data Governance program. They provide the procedures and standards for consistency and discipline in Data Management processes. By the time you are ready to write policies, you have most of the inputs from a roles and responsibilities perspective. Keep the policies concise so users understand what is expected of them but not so strict that they cannot or will not be followed. Policies can also be developed by formalizing Data Management activities that are already working. Take the time to write those things down so new stakeholder onboarding will be smoother. Lastly, measure compliance even if you are not there yet. It might take time, but you can always take making progress toward compliance as a win for your program.

CHAPTER **14**

Data Governance Maturity

RESULTS YOU CAN EXPECT WITH MATURITY

As Data Governance matures in the organization, stakeholders will realize the benefits of the program. If we go back to the common challenges outlined in the "Introduction," such benefits might include the following (Table 14.1):

Table 14.1 Benefits Realization.

Challenge	Realization
Metadata	• Having common definitions of business terms • Consolidated and current data dictionary
Access to Data	• Availability of common tools • Knowledge of what data is available for use and where to get it
Trust in Data	• More time to analyze and make actionable business decisions
Data Integration	• Access to data that has already been integrated • Reduced reliance on desktop tools to cull and merge data together to make it presentable • Common tools to centralize both integration and business rules
Data Ownership	• Access to the name of the individual who can help when there are questions about data
Reporting/Analytics	• Relevant context to data available in reports or datasets • Common tools that are appropriate for different users
Data Architecture	• Consistency of column names across tables • Access to a data model
Reliance on Individual Knowledge	• Understanding where to find information on common processes • Removing the need to call an individual because they have always been willing to help
Culture	• Ability to gain access to data historically siloed by division or department • Excitement in maturing data capabilities

These are just some examples of benefits and this list is not exhaustive. Your organization may realize entirely different benefits. The following section is a recap of what we have explored in each of the previous chapters as we think about how to mature Data Governance.

DATA GOVERNANCE MATURITY CYCLE

Sustainable Data Governance programs are not one-shot efforts (clean up and move on). To achieve the best results, successful programs identify the organizational processes behind Data Management and identify desired outcomes; the Data Governance program becomes part of the daily routine and is embedded in the culture of the organization.

There are five distinct stages that an organization transitions through as they embark on and then mature in their Data Governance journey. The journey does not end but continues in a repeating cycle as the needs of the business change. The exact reason for any one organization to embark on the Data Governance journey may differ but the keys to success are consistent.

Each of the steps in the Data Governance Maturity Cycle (see Figure 14.1) are an integral part of establishing and — more importantly — sustaining a Data Governance program. The initial steps are linear but then proceed in a cyclical fashion over time as it is imperative to revisit changing needs and solutions. Crucially, the cycle lays out a path for natural maturation and growth in the future. The five distinct stages of the Data Governance Maturity Cycle are:

1. Define Program
2. Identify Challenges
3. Develop Policy
4. Policy Execution
5. Monitor and Measure

Stage 1 – Define Program

Successful Data Governance programs share a common thread — the program champions have taken the time to define the following:

Initial Focus

As with any problem, the first step to resolution is defining what "it" is and designing an approach to solving "it." Take the time to think about what you need to start solving for in the short term. Focus can always shift; in fact, that is a sign of maturity.

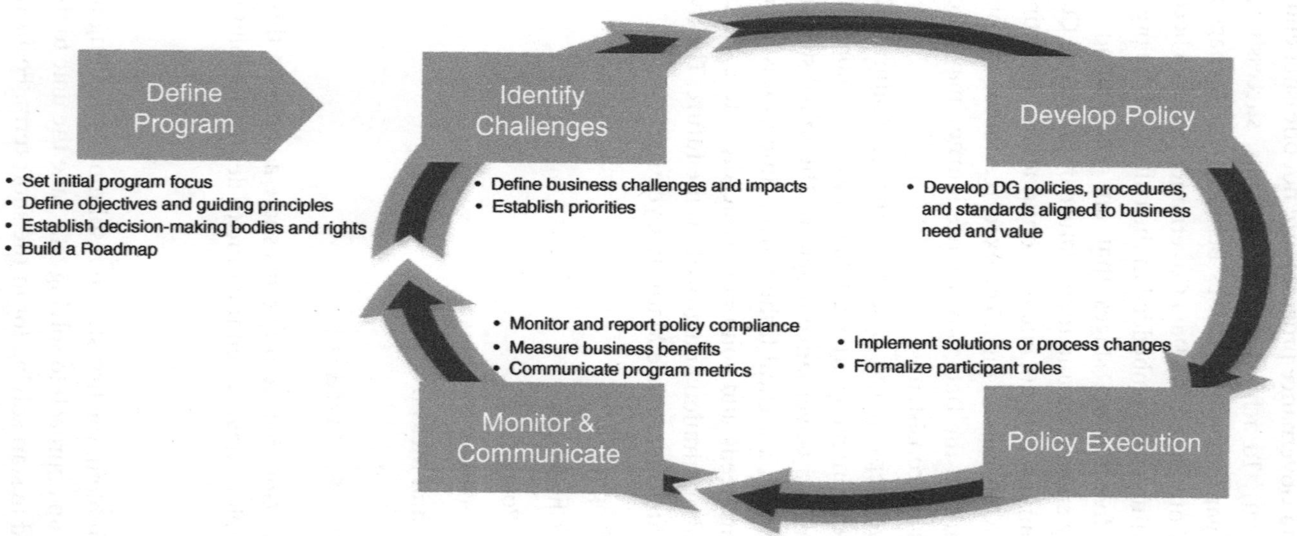
Define Program
Set initial program focus
Define objectives and guiding principles
Establish decision-making bodies and rights
Build a Roadmap
Identify Challenges
Define business challenges and impacts
Establish priorities
Develop Policy
Develop DG policies, procedures, and standards aligned to business need and value
Policy Execution
Implement solutions or process changes
Formalize participant roles
Monitor & Communicate
Monitor and report policy compliance
Measure business benefits
Communicate program metrics

Figure 14.1 Data Governance Maturity Cycle.

If you are still having trouble trying to figure out that initial focus, take another look at Chapter 1, Introduction, and then perhaps align your challenges to the different Data Stewardship models found in Chapter 7, Organizational Framework. Think about data-related challenges that impact master domains, a department, a business process, or a project. Use that as your focus to get the program started.

Remember not to start with too many Data Governance entry points. If you do, the program will become overwhelmed. This was covered in Chapter 5, Common Starting Points.

Program Objectives and Guiding Principles

By now, you have a pretty good understanding that defining objectives is an important cornerstone of any Data Governance program. If you have done everything else recommended and still do not have program objectives, take a step back and write them down. You need them to solve for your challenges in a disciplined and methodical manner. They will also help you when you need to communicate program activity and measurement.

Along with the objectives, define your guiding principles to set some lines in the sand about how your program will operate. They really do make a good touchpoint if participants do not remember why a decision was made.

See Chapter 6, Data Governance Planning, Chapter 10, Communication, and Chapter 11, Measurement, for examples of objectives, guiding principles, a communication strategy, and how to build a program scorecard.

Decision-Making Bodies

Program participants will need to understand where they fit into the overall program structure and what they will be asked to do. At the end of the day, you really just need to start by drawing a picture of the organizational framework and describing at a high level what the different bodies will be asked to do. Do this without thinking about the names of the people who may be asked to fill the structure. There are several samples of organizational structures in Chapter 7, Organizational Framework.

As you build out the program's structure, you also need to design how the program is going to operate. Thinking about this ahead of onboarding participants will help with the onboarding and training process. Participants, especially reluctant ones, will be more likely to become active participants if they understand their role and how the role may impact their other job responsibilities (and their calendar). There is more information in Chapter 9, Operating Procedures.

Decision Rights

In order to ensure program participants are at the right level in the organization to make decisions, you need to understand at a detailed level what the different "asks" are from each group. Remember to start with your program objectives and then define the activities and/ or decisions. After that, assign "responsible," "accountable," "consulted," or "informed" (RACI matrix). The "accountable" assignments need to be roles with the proper level of authority. See the Roles and Responsibilities to revisit how to build the RACI matrix and eventually name participants.

Roadmap

You have defined scope, objectives, guiding principles, the organizational framework, and roles and responsibilities. What's next? You need to define the plan for how to operationalize the program. That means you need a roadmap. The roadmap will not only help you execute the program but also serves as a communication and measurement tool. See Chapter 12, Roadmap, for roadmap layout examples, the right level of detail, and when to think about formality.

Stage 2 – Identify Challenges

If you are at the very beginning of your Data Governance journey, this becomes a validation step with the onboarded Data Governance participants (the Data Owners in our example) because you just did it while you were defining your program. Depending on the scope of Data Governance, the Data Owner may decide on some challenges that need to be addressed within the context of their domain. In other words, things that may not have an impact on the enterprise. When you are at the beginning, it is always recommended to tackle one problem that is large enough to make an impact but small enough to be achievable in a relatively short amount of time.

As you repeat the cycle, it is important to reassess what potential new focus areas need to be identified by your challenges and established priorities. Requests, questions, new projects, and issues will always arise. Keep consistent about priorities. Reread Chapter 4, Priorities, as a reminder. There are examples of workflows for priorities and intake in Chapter 9, Operating Procedures. Those workflows were developed straight from the RACI exercise in Chapter 8, Roles and Responsibilities.

Stage 3 – Develop Policy

Policy development is the heart of the Data Governance program. Policies define the approach for Data Management and the expected outcomes. Policies can be developed to solve for any number of challenges including definitions, data quality, master data, data security, data modeling, data naming, or data integration.

The policy itself is merely a set of statements intended to define how to manage or use data. They are then made up of procedures that provide policy implementation instructions and standards that define the required configuration for the policy. The policies themselves can be broad in that they focus on more of an enterprise level (e.g., data naming standards, standard data quality process) or more granular in nature (e.g., department level hierarchy structure).

Regardless of the reach of the policy, it is recommended to be consistent with the layout and contents of each policy. Participants should not have to wade through different documentation depending on the data domain, department, or even different authors. The Program Management function can help ensure consistency from a template perspective.

Policy authors tend to be participants assigned to Data Steward roles working in conjunction with data domain or business process subject matter experts. In our organizational framework example, this would have been a Working Group assigned by a Data Owner. Depending on the policy to be developed, these roles may be filled by either the business and IT team or a combination of both. For example, a product hierarchy would be developed with a business focus while database naming standards would be developed with an IT focus.

There is a sample policy table of contents along with policy examples for data quality and metadata in Chapter 4, Policies. There is also a sample workflow of policy development and approval in Chapter 9, Operating Procedures.

Drafting and approving a policy is the easy part, but there is no value in simply developing a policy. In fact, a policy with no measurable outcome is truly an academic exercise. Programs that get stuck in this stage are doomed to fail. You need to be able to move to the fourth stage to realize the outcomes.

Stage 4 – Policy Execution

This is the stage where that realization occurs. The Data Management team, IT partner, or business areas can now deliver solutions to facilitate compliance to the stated policies and procedures. Achieving compliance to policies may include a wide range of changes from organizational structure, business processes, applications, or even the introduction of new technologies. There may also be some combination of each of these.

While stated succinctly above, the level of effort involved in moving your organization toward compliance should not be underestimated. Other than policies that reflect and formalize current operations, any other compliance will require a change management process for ongoing adoption. Data Governance stakeholders, sponsors, and champions also need to remember that depending on the scope of the change needed, compliance will not happen overnight. Another consideration is competition with all the other projects and initiatives in the organization. The Data Governance program may need to justify their needs just like the other departments or programs vying for limited resources. That is another reason that alignment to overall business objectives is so important. The key is to plan for change, and both monitor and communicate progress.

Stage 5 – Monitor and Communicate

In the last stage of the cycle, you are not only monitoring ongoing compliance to developed policies but also measuring their actual outcomes against the desired outcomes, in other words, the stated objectives. There are two types of monitoring to consider. The first is at the policy level. Each policy should define what compliance means and how it needs to be monitored. See Chapter 13, Policies, for sample policies that include measurement. The second type of monitoring is at the program level. This is measurement against the stated program objectives. See Chapter 11, Measurement, for more information on creating a program scorecard.

While you begin to measure your program, you also need to communicate. Communication is imperative so leadership understands progress, and stakeholders not involved in day-to-day program operations understand processes and outcomes. Various communications need to be defined along with the cadence. Once a communications plan is defined, you need to stick to the plan. If you tell senior leadership you are going to produce a program scorecard on a quarterly basis, produce a program scorecard monthly. If you do not, stakeholders will begin to question the validity and importance of Data Governance processes. See Chapter 10, Communication, for different ideas on what types of communications to produce.

MATURING YOUR PROGRAM

Once you have completed the final stage, you are not done. That is why we call it a "cycle." You begin the process over again. Your program is maturing when you are moving through the stages with greater frequency. When you are doing that, your program is expanding.

It can also be said that you do not have to only focus on one stage at a time before starting the cycle over again. You may find you have multiple "markers" in different stages. That is okay and expected. Again, start with one focus first. Once you begin to monitor and communicate, it is expected to move on to the next thing (i.e., issue, question, challenge, project) to be addressed. Remember there is no time frame on policy compliance.

SUMMARY

Every customer I have worked with agrees that Data Governance will provide value to their organization. But Data Governance programs continue to struggle in gaining traction or being sustainable over the long haul. The programs are often seen as yet more bureaucratic overhead in how people get their jobs done with ever pressing deadlines and what feels like fewer resources. It will never cease to amaze me that people always seem to find the time to fight the fires and live in chaos instead of figuring out to contain them or not set them in the first place.

I have outlined how Data Governance can help solve for Data Management challenges that impact all areas of the business by:

- outlining a process to define and implement a Data Governance program.
- providing examples that can be used as templates for any program that is trying to get off the ground.
- offering a cycle for maturing Data Governance.

The first step is really to acknowledge the need and garner the interest and support of someone in your organization with the right level of decision-making authority. It only takes one.

Also, do not let the attempt at perfection keep you from getting started. You cannot sit down and think about every scenario in your organization and how you would address it. Start with something that will provide value and expand from there. Keep the cycle going, and you will enjoy the benefits of more disciplined Data Management practices, whether that is a better understanding of your customers and how they interact with your products or services, compliance to internal or external mandates, the ability to expand your business, getting faster at decision making through trust in reports and datasets, or achieving operational efficiencies by reducing costs or getting work done faster. It can be done.

In closing, a customer once asked me when they would be done with Data Governance. You are never done. Data Governance is a journey that continues as long as there are data needs and a desire to utilize that data to its full potential. Good luck on your own journey!

About the Author

Mary Anne Hopper is a Senior Manager who oversees the SAS Management and Advisory Consulting practice. She has over 20 years of experience helping clients develop as well as execute strategies in the areas of data governance, data management, master data management, and reporting and analytics. Her global experience has covered numerous industries and data subject areas including financial services, retail, education, government, manufacturing, partner management, website analytics, supply chain management, and health and life sciences.

Mary Anne is a co-author of the *SAS Data Management Framework* and *SAS Data Governance Maturity Model*.

Glossary of Terms

Term	Definition
Business Data Portfolio	A top-of-mind list of reporting and analytical capabilities for measuring and improving business outcomes that is aligned to data subject areas creating a foundation for establishing cross-functional priority for development activities. The Portfolio helps to promote the reuse of data assets.
Business Rule	A definition of how data should be treated to reflect business definitions or how the business operates.
Business Sponsor	Business executive responsible for defining enterprise strategies and objectives for data usage, promoting, and funding the DG program and encouraging adoption.
Business Stakeholder	Individuals or groups with a vested interest in the final product; a group or individuals that have a vested interest in or are affected by the outcome of a decision concerning data practices or definitions.
Data Administration	Data Management capability defined as the day-to-day administration of data and databases.
Data Architecture	Data Management capability defined as the models, policies, rules, and standards about what data is captured, how it is stored, arranged, and integrated (includes data analysis, data modeling, data design).
Data Governance Program Management	The Program Management function ensures that DG is executing consistently and effectively across focus areas. The team will also communicate performance indicators and program metrics across the divisions.
Data Governance Steering Committee	The purpose of the DG Steering Committee is to provide strategic guidance and foster a cooperative environment to support DG execution. Their guidance will ensure city-wide acceptance of DG and support the long-term sustainability of the DG program. This is a permanent group comprised of executive leadership.
Data Life Cycle	Data Management capability that defines how data and information are created, stored, distributed, used, maintained, archived, and disposed.
Data Management	The tactical execution of data governance policies and standards. Data management encompasses those activities (including data architecture, metadata, data quality, privacy, and security) responsible for rigorously managing BNY's critical data assets on a day-to-day basis.

(Continued)

Term	Definition
Data Owner Team Member	The Data Owner Team is a group of key stakeholders that represent data in support of a given focus area. They will have the authority to make decisions about the data and create working teams of business and IT individuals to effectively resolve issues. The group will also direct the work of Data Stewards.
Data Quality	Data Management capability defined the conformance of data to the business definitions and the business rules (i.e., business metadata). It should be noted that data without business metadata has no defined quality.
Data Security	Data Management capability that defines how data is accessed, secured, and privacy is handled.
Data Steward	Resource accountable for gathering information requirements and defining standards and rules to ensure data is compliant with defined information policies and quality requirements within their assigned domain.
Data Stewardship Teams	Data Stewards leverage their business and technical knowledge of business processes, data domains, and integration points to identify data quality issues, develop business rules and definitions, identify compliance issues, and make policy recommendations.
[Enterprise] Data Governance	Also referred to by the abbreviation EDG. It is the organizing framework for establishing a business strategy, objectives, and policies for shared data. Data governance ensures data is managed as an enterprise asset by assigning accountability and authority for decision making around data and ensuring business practices comply with established policies.
Metadata	Data Management capability defined as the capture, storage, documentation, and publishing of information about enterprise data such as its description, lineage, usage, ownership, etc.
Policy	A rule, law, or regulation that serves as a statement of intent designed to influence and determine decisions or a course of action.
Procedure	A document containing steps that specify how to perform a process.
Reference & Master Data	Data Management capability defined as the practices and processes used to manage key business reference data. Master data domains include citizens, programs, locations, and so on. Master data is typically shared or referenced by multiple business processes and systems, requiring a coordinated approach to their creation, management, and use.
Reporting & Analytics	Data Management capability that reflects the proper management of data in reporting and analytics, including ETL, data mining, BI, EDW, and data marts.
Standard	A set of criteria for a process, activity, or object against which a result or compliance can be assessed. Policies may require adherence to particular standards.
Subject Matter Expert (SME)	Business or technical resource with in-depth knowledge and expertise about the context and use of information within business processes or application systems. SMEs may include business analysts, data architects, data analysts, and so on.

Index